# The Emotions

The emotions are at the center of our lives and, for better or worse, imbue them with much of their significance. The philosophical problems stirred up by the existence of the emotions, over which many great philosophers of the past have labored, revolve around attempts to understand what this significance amounts to. Are emotions feelings, thoughts, or experiences? If they are experiences, what are they experiences of? Are emotions rational? In what sense do emotions give meaning to what surrounds us? *The Emotions: A Philosophical Introduction* introduces and explores these questions in a clear and accessible way. The authors discuss the following key topics:

- the diversity and unity of the emotions;
- the relations between emotion, belief, and desire;
- the nature of values;
- the relations between emotions and perceptions;
- emotions viewed as evaluative attitudes;
- the link between emotions and evaluative knowledge;
- the nature of moods, sentiments, and character traits.

Including chapter summaries and guides to further reading, *The Emotions: A Philosophical Introduction* is an ideal starting point for any philosopher or student studying the emotions. It will also be of interest to those in related disciplines such as psychology and the social sciences.

**Julien A. Deonna** is Assistant Professor at the Department of Philosophy of the University of Geneva (Switzerland) and at the Swiss Centre for Research in the Affective Sciences. He works on theories of emotions and moral psychology. He is co-author of *In Defense of Shame* (Oxford University Press, 2011).

**Fabrice Teroni** is Postdoctoral Assistant at the Philosophy Department at Bern University (Switzerland) and Senior Researcher at the Swiss Centre for Research in the Affective Sciences. He works on theories of emotions and memory. He is co-author of *Defense of Shame* (Oxford University Press, 2011).

# The Emotions

## A philosophical introduction

Julien A. Deonna and Fabrice Teroni

Routledge
Taylor & Francis Group

LONDON AND NEW YORK

This edition published 2012
by Routledge
2 Park Square, Milton Park, Abingdon, Oxon, OX14 4RN

Simultaneously published in the USA and Canada
by Routledge
711 Third Avenue, New York, NY 10017

*Routledge is an imprint of the Taylor & Francis Group, an informa business*

Julien A. Deonna, Fabrice Teroni, *Qu'est-ce qu'une émotion?*
© Librairie Philosophique J. Vrin, Paris, 2008.
http://www.vrin.fr

*British Library Cataloguing in Publication Data*
A catalogue record for this book is available from the British Library

*Library of Congress Cataloging-in-Publication Data*
Deonna, Julien A.
[Qu'est-ce qu'une émotion? English]
The emotions : a philosophical introduction / by Julien A. Deonna and Fabrice Teroni.
p. cm.
Includes bibliographical references (p. ) and index.
ISBN 978-0-415-61492-4 (hardback : alk. paper) -- ISBN 978-0-415-61493-1
(pbk. : alk. paper) 1. Emotions (Philosophy) I. Teroni, Fabrice. II. Title.
B105.E46D4613 2011
128'.37--dc23
2011038856

ISBN13: 978-0-415-61492-4 (hbk)
ISBN13: 978-0-415-61493-1 (pbk)

Typeset in Garamond
by Taylor & Francis Books

# Contents

# Acknowledgements

This book is the intellectual offspring of a short introductory essay on the nature of emotions we wrote in French under the title *Qu'est-ce qu'une émotion?* published a few years ago with Vrin. While pleased with what we had achieved, we soon realized that numerous gaps had to be filled and that many of the topics considered and arguments pursued required further clarification and elaboration. The present essay, which we strangely thought would be a slightly revised translation of the original, is essentially a new book, despite the fact that it shares with its ancestor part of its basic structure, arguments, and general approach to the emotions. We express our gratitude to Vrin for having welcomed the present project.

In the process of writing this book, we have benefited immensely from our very stimulating working environment within the Swiss National Centre of Competence in Research in the Affective Sciences at the University of Geneva, and in particular within Thumos, its research group in the philosophy of the emotions. We would like to thank its core members, Otto Bruun, Thomas Cochrane, Anita Konzelmann Ziv, Federico Lauria, Olivier Massin, Kevin Mulligan, Alain Pé-Curto, Raffaele Rodogno, and Cain Todd for their invaluable help. Our gratitude extends also to the following people for their precious remarks, advice, and kindness over the years: Monika Betzler, Michael Brady, Fabrice Clément, Ronald de Sousa, Jérôme Dokic, Sabine Döring, Julien Dutant, Pascal Engel, Richard Glauser, Bennett Helm, Dale Jacquette, Laurence Kauffmann, Philipp Keller, Anita Konzelmann Ziv, Stéphane Lemaire, Pierre Livet, Anne Meylan, Adam Morton, Bence Nanay, Isabelle Pitteloud, David Sander, Klaus Scherer, Gianfranco Soldati, and Emma Tieffenbach.

Our thinking has also been enriched by the questions of our students and the numerous discussions we have had with them on the topics covered in this book at the Universities of Bern, Geneva, Lausanne, and Neuchâtel. Thanks to all of them.

The following people have read the whole or parts of previous versions of this book: Philip Gerrans, Federico Lauria, Olivier Massin, Kevin Mulligan, Mikko Salmela, Christine Tappolet, and Edoardo Zamuner. Their comments and criticisms have been decisive. We cannot thank them enough for the generosity and care they have displayed in their engagement with our work. Our deepest gratitude goes to Kevin Mulligan, who first aroused our interest in the emotions and who, through his encouragement, has been a constant source of stimulation in the sharpening of our ideas. Our most important debt is to Otto Bruun. We owe the readability of this book to his work on earlier drafts. More importantly, his comments, suggestions, and objections have not only helped us avoid numerous mistakes, they have also contributed immensely to improving the quality of our presentation. Finally, we want to acknowledge here all that we owe to Peter Goldie for his kindness and generosity as a friend, the support and stimulation he offered to younger philosophers, and the inspiring example and infectious enthusiasm he provided as an original thinker. He died while our work on this book was coming to a close. We will miss him dearly.

# Preface

The present book is an introduction to the philosophy of the emotions and as such presents and assesses the major theories of what the emotions are, as well as the numerous issues that the significant and growing interest in them has brought to light in recent years. It would perhaps have been possible to provide this introductory overview of the theoretical landscape from a detached distance, but this is a route we have deliberately chosen not to follow. Instead, we have opted to lead the reader on a ground-level trek through the intellectual thickets of the current debates in the field, taking sides and staking out positions as we advance. This book is, as a result, a very opinionated introduction.

This is not the only reason why this introduction is distinctive and why it may claim to fill a gap in the flurry of recent publications on the emotions. First, it is throughout informed by many broader discussions and debates central to contemporary philosophy of mind and epistemology. The phenomenology and intentionality of the emotions, as well as epistemological issues surrounding them, are considered from the perspective of these debates as they are conducted in the current literature. Second, while the book works its way towards a satisfactory account of the emotions, it also tries to make up for the relative neglect that has attended the rest of our affective lives. Thus, we furnish accounts of emotional dispositions, moods, temperaments, character traits, and sentiments and examine their various roles in connection with the emotions. Third and finally, the much dissected connection between emotions and values or evaluative properties is subjected to a degree of scrutiny unusual for a textbook. This is not only because we think that clarifying this connection is essential for an understanding of the nature of emotions, but also because it informs crucial philosophical debates raised by their study, namely those surrounding the metaphysics of values and the nature of our evaluative knowledge. The shape and relevance of these debates for the general philosophy of the emotions is also something we have sought to convey.

Before we present the structure of the book, let us make a few remarks regarding our use of notes and references. The knowledgeable reader will be struck by the scarcity of the former. We have indeed kept notes to a minimum in order to avoid distractions from the main threads of the arguments we discuss. While we have put what we perceive as the principal references in the main body of the text, we have been rather conservative in doing so, again with the aim of maximizing the readability of a text that can, due to the complexity of the material, at times be challenging. The drawbacks of these choices are, we hope, made up for in the 'Questions and further readings' sections at the end of each chapter. In those sections, we furnish the resources to pursue in greater depth the main themes and lines of inquiry in the broader literature.

We shall now briefly present how our discussion is structured. We start by emphasizing three fundamental features of the emotions: it feels a certain way to have an emotion, emotions are about something, and we assess emotions from a variety of different perspectives. The issues raised by these features of the emotions – their phenomenology, their intentionality, and their epistemological significance – constitute the core material on which this book is built. Introducing these three features is the principal purpose of Chapter 1, which in this way provides a first insight into the nature of emotions and allows us to contrast them with other types of psychological phenomena, in particular other types of affective phenomena.

Chapter 2 introduces a series of distinctions commonly drawn within the class of emotions. There are for instance positive and negative emotions, conscious and unconscious emotions, reflexive and non-reflexive emotions. We turn our attention to the significance of these distinctions, and offer a closely argued critique of a recent and important brand of skepticism regarding the very unity of the class of emotions, a skepticism fostered by another of these distinctions – that between basic and nonbasic emotions.

In Chapter 3, we investigate the first group of theories about what the emotions are, theories that claim emotions are reducible to admixtures of beliefs and desires. While presenting some of the classical reasons for which these various theories have been found wanting, we also show, through a deeper understanding of the nature of desires, why, ultimately, the fact that emotions motivate us in all sorts of ways does not support the idea that they should be understood in terms of desires.

Theories of the emotions that do not appeal to desires have generally approached them through their connections with values. The remainder of the book assesses theories of the emotions that conceive of them as specific forms of evaluation. Chapter 4 looks at the connection between evaluative properties and emotional responses and, more centrally, the metaphysical nature of evaluative properties. We thus review different positions on the nature of these properties, from the strongest forms of subjectivism to various forms of objectivism. We conclude that there are good reasons to think that these properties are independent of our emotional responses.

In Chapter 5, we focus on theories according to which emotions are evaluative judgments. We discuss numerous ways in which one might try to salvage this classical and intellectualist portrayal of the emotions. One strategy involves complementing the intellectual judgment with a further layer of feelings (add-on theories). Another regards emotions as inchoate feelings given form by intellectual fiat (reversed add-on or constructionist theories). All these theories, we argue, fail to account for the distinctive role of phenomenology within the emotions.

By contrast, perceptual theories of the emotions can reasonably claim to be giving the phenomenological aspect of emotions its due weight, in viewing them as perceptual experiences of evaluative properties. Chapter 6 investigates the credentials of this presently very influential family of approaches to the emotions. In reviewing various and more or less elaborate forms of the perceptual theory, which lay more or less emphasis on the role of bodily feelings in emotion, we suggest that all of them face serious worries. While this discussion helps us bring into sharper focus the basic constraints a satisfactory theory of the emotions has to meet – regarding their phenomenology, their intentionality and their epistemological role – the perceptual analogy is, we conclude, more misleading than enlightening.

On the basis of the various difficulties attending the theories we find in the contemporary philosophical literature on the emotions, Chapter 7 lays out a novel account, one which we claim satisfies the basic constraints that our discussion of the preceding chapters has helped uncover. The otherwise mysterious connection between emotions and evaluative properties, we suggest, is brought to the surface by leveraging a distinction between attitudes and their content. Unlike all the other theories that lay emphasis on this connection, we argue that evaluative properties do not figure in the content of the emotions. Instead, this connection is grounded in the attitudinal component specific to each emotion type. We develop this approach by appealing to the idea that emotions are felt stances towards objects, and explain how it accounts for the intimate link between the distinctive intentionality and phenomenology of the emotions.

The three last chapters of the book are structured around the epistemological issues raised by the emotions and aim to assess their role in the acquisition of evaluative knowledge. Chapter 8 investigates the conditions that have to be met in order for an emotion to be justified. Justified emotions, we argue, do not depend on any antecedent cognition of evaluative properties: they can be justified by non-evaluative states such as perceptions, memories, or factual beliefs. Consequently they need not be mere reactions to prior evaluative knowledge or belief and can thus play a fundamental role in our access to the evaluative domain. Although we conduct our discussion from within the framework of our own theory of the emotions, the conclusions we reach are largely independent of it.

Chapter 9 focuses on the roles that affective and/or motivational states such as moods, sentiments, character traits, and desires play in regard to the emotions. We provide detailed descriptions of these states, examine the fundamental roles they play in causing and influencing emotions and contrast these roles with another we might think they play, i.e. that of providing reasons for emotional episodes. We present and criticize some important arguments for the latter view – and conclude that they do not contribute positively to the justification of emotions.

The final chapter looks at the importance of emotions in regard to evaluative knowledge. More specifically, it investigates whether there exists a safe epistemological route going from the emotions to the evaluative judgments they tend to elicit and how this route compares with others ending in the same judgments but bypassing the emotions altogether. We conclude with an account of why the emotional route has a very special significance in the acquisition of evaluative knowledge.

# 1   Homing in on the emotions

The philosophy of emotions seeks to develop a systematic theory of the phenomena we refer to by terms such as 'fear', 'envy', 'anger', 'sadness', 'joy', 'embarrassment', 'shame', 'jealousy', 'remorse', 'boredom', 'nostalgia', 'pride', 'regret', 'admiration', 'compassion', 'disgust', 'amusement', 'indignation', 'hope', which fall under the generic label of 'emotions'. We know it when we are undergoing emotions, often we know which emotion we have, and we know how to ascribe them to others and why we ascribe them. Still, the fact that this intuitive knowledge is easily available should not make us think that emotions are simple phenomena. Let us start, then, by introducing what are often thought to be the central features of the emotions, features we shall illustrate by considering how the emotions contrast with other affective phenomena and, more generally, other psychological states. Doing so will not only furnish some preliminary insights into the nature of emotions, but will also put us in a position to briefly present some of the main issues with which we shall be concerned in this book. The first of these core features concerns the role of feelings in the emotions (their phenomenology), the second the fact that emotions are directed towards objects (their intentionality), and the third the sorts of standards to which the emotions are answerable (their epistemology).

## Phenomenology

Consider the following everyday expressions: we say we are 'in the grip of panic', 'struck by fear', 'overcome with joy', 'oppressed by shame', 'overwhelmed by sorrow'. These locutions suggest that emotions are reactions we passively undergo. The term 'passion', which used to refer to what are now known as emotions, testifies to that fact. So are the many participial adjectives designating emotions (e.g., 'horrified', 'astonished', 'troubled', 'vexed'). In the emotions, we seem to be acted on, and this typically manifests itself to us through bodily agitations or disturbances – a feature to which the very term 'emotion' alludes. The crucial point for present purposes, however, is that these bodily disturbances are felt. This is why the term 'feeling' is never far away when there is talk of the emotions.

What are these bodily disturbances or agitations that we are said to be feeling during emotional episodes? Emotions are generally held to involve bodily sensations or feelings. Anger, for example, may lend itself to a description in terms of a configuration of sensations caused *inter alia* by the following elements: an accelerating heart rate, quickened breathing, an increased blood pressure, a rush of adrenaline. Such descriptions will also refer to the sorts of kinesthetic sensations and muscular feedback characteristic of the particular emotion that is experienced – compare for instance the muscular relaxation in relief with the muscular tension typical of anger. To the kinds of sensations just described, we may also add the sensations of pleasure and displeasure often referred to as hedonic qualities or tones. There are after all emotions that feel good, like joy or admiration, and others that do not, like fear or sadness.

More generally, and independently of any specification of how their felt character should be described, the emotions are said to have a phenomenology: there is a 'what-it-is-like'-ness to the experience of any emotion. This seems to be what we are referring to when we talk generally of 'the feeling of anger' or 'the feeling of shame'. Now, while it is easy to approach the phenomenology of the emotions through its dimension of bodily disturbance, it goes without saying that felt agitations of the body do not seem to be particularly salient in the phenomenology of many emotions – think for instance of regret or contentment. Similarly, the idea that all emotions are intrinsically either pleasant or unpleasant is less than straightforward. While many think that anger is unpleasant and that hope is pleasant, this is far from obvious. To complicate matters further, the phenomenology of the emotions might lend itself to very different descriptions depending on whether the subject's attention is focused on what he feels or is directed elsewhere, for instance on the situation that triggers his emotion.

An important task we shall take up in this book then concerns the role and nature of feelings, especially bodily and hedonic feelings, within emotions. The fact that phenomenology is a central feature of the emotions is reflected in the fact that just knowing that someone is angry, afraid or ashamed is already to be in possession of a substantial amount of psychological information about him, and this is so even when one does not know what he is angry about, afraid or ashamed of (e.g., Roberts 2003: 146). Yet, can we identify the emotions with some aspect of their felt character, be it bodily sensations or hedonic tones? These issues, and more generally the question as to how we should conceive of the phenomenology of the emotions and its roles, will be the center of our discussions in Chapters 6 and 7. As we shall see, while there have been many attempts to identify emotions with phenomenological features; these attempts seem to rule out the possibility of unfelt emotions and run the risk of placing too much emphasis on the qualities of the emotional experience itself at the expense of what these experiences are experiences of. Indeed, while it is true that the emotions are affective phenomena that seem to be partly characterized by what it is like to have them, another of their central features consists in the fact that they are directed towards various aspects of the world. It is to this central feature of the emotions that we now turn.

## Intentionality

We said that emotions are reactions. This raises the question as to what they are reactions to. A good starting point is to consider the way we speak of the emotions. A cursory overview of our linguistic practices in this area brings to light the fact that emotions seem to be always about something. One can always ask, for instance, *what* Bernard is angry about (e.g., 'he is angry at Arthur because he insulted him'), *what* he is afraid of (e.g., 'a stock-market crash'), *who* he is jealous of (e.g., 'Max, who is dating Mary'). This is part of what philosophers have in mind when they call emotions *intentional* phenomena. This is simply a term of art for saying that the emotions are about something, and should not be understood as suggesting that they are states we deliberately or intentionally enter into. Rather, as we have seen, the opposite seems to be the case. It is worth observing that claiming that emotions have intentional objects in the sense just defined is not, or not merely, to claim that they have causes or triggers. While the object of an emotion is also often its cause, it does not have to be. The object of Bernard's jealousy is Max, but its cause is, say, Mary's praise of Max's humor. Note as well that to say that emotions always have objects is not to say that these objects are the focus of attention for the duration of the emotion – John is worried about his exam, but his attention is presently focused on checking whether his bike is locked – nor even that the subject is always clear about what these objects are, as we shall see in our discussion of the various senses in which emotions can be said to be unconscious in Chapter 2.

The language of emotions also reveals that they can have different sorts of objects. This is reflected in the fact that emotion-related verbs can take a variety of grammatical complements. Take the following examples: 'Bernard fears that his life is in danger', 'Mary hopes that the economy will improve', 'Alison regrets that Jacob did not come to the party'. In these three cases, the emotion-related verb is followed by a propositional complement. However, there are also cases such as 'Bernard fears the lion', 'Mary admires Max', and 'Jeffrey despises sexists', where the verb takes a nominal complement. Although most emotion verbs can take either nominal or propositional complements, there are some notable exceptions: 'admire' standardly requires a direct object, and 'hope' a that-clause. It is often easy to transform a construction involving a propositional complement into one with a nominal complement ('Bernard fears for his life', 'Mary hopes for an improvement in the economy'), but transformations in the other direction are often not possible. For example, sentences of the form 'Mary admires the fact that Max is/did F' are not only grammatically infelicitous, but it is not clear that Mary's admiration for Max could be captured in terms of a single proposition, or even a collection of propositions.

These features of the language of emotions reflect the rich variety of the emotions' intentional objects. In some cases, the emotions are or even have to be attitudes towards specific states of affairs, e.g., regret. In other cases, they are attitudes we take towards specific objects or events that do not seem reducible to an attitude taken towards a state of affairs involving that object, or a collection of such states. Beliefs, but – as we shall see – also desires, do not seem to exhibit the same richness.

Now, whatever type of object emotions have, the fact that they always have one helps distinguish them from another very important class of affective phenomena, i.e. moods. Moods, like emotions, have a characteristic phenomenology. There clearly is something it is like to be in a downcast or a grumpy mood. And, while moods typically last longer than emotions, they need not always do so. Unlike emotions, however, and this is the principled distinction between these two types of affective phenomena, moods do not appear to be intentional in that they never target specific objects. This is why it does not make sense to restrict the attribution of a mood to specific objects or kinds of objects. One is in a gloomy, grumpy or joyful mood, never gloomy or grumpy about Mike or about the rich. This is reflected in the fact that attributions of moods (e.g., Alison is grumpy) are informative and complete without specification of any object, whereas attributions of emotions (e.g., Alison is angry) may, as we have seen, be informative but remain incomplete as long as the object is not specified. Of course, as the standard metaphor goes, our moods 'color' our attitudes in general, and have close connections with emotions in particular, which complicates matters further. Moods often cause emotions (and vice-versa) of the same affective color (someone in a bad mood will tend to feel mainly negative emotions) and moods commonly crystallize in the form of emotional episodes that will target specific objects (Alison's grumpiness does not have Mike as an object but may well lead to her being angry at him). Similarly, grumpiness may be the result of a series of negative emotions.

If emotions differ from moods in virtue of being intentionally directed at specific objects, how do they come to have the objects they have? A first observation is that emotions can equally well be directed at objects, events, or states of affairs with which the subject is presently in perceptual contact ('Ben is afraid of this lion'), with which she had previously been in perceptual contact ('Mary regrets having met Ben in the Jungle'), with which she has never been in such contact ('Louis is disappointed that Napoleon lost the Battle of Waterloo'), and also with states of affairs with which perceptual contact is impossible ('Rebecca hopes she will travel to Atlantis'). Here we have an important difference between emotions and perceptions. Perceptions are answerable to a causal constraint according to which the perceived objects and properties have to be causally responsible for the occurrence of the perceptual experience. Sam sees the blueness of this vase only if this vase and its blueness cause his visual experience. When such a constraint is not satisfied, he does not see the vase but only *seems* to see it. And this does not seem true in the case of emotions, or at least certainly not true of all of them. Do we want to say for instance that Ben only seems to be afraid if he has mistaken Bernard passing in a bedsheet for a ghost?[1]

In answer to the question of how emotions come to have the objects they have, we must then acknowledge, and this is our second observation, that there is no generic answer to that question, for emotions necessarily rely on other mental states in order to be intentionally directed at something. Emotions, unlike perceptions, are always grounded in some other mental state that is also about the object the emotion is directed at. Perception gives us direct access to the relevant objects and facts in the sense that it does not call for the presence of another mental state directed at these very objects and facts, whereas emotions must latch on to information provided by other mental states. And these mental states, which we shall call the *cognitive bases* of emotions, can be of radically different types.

This is reflected in the fact that emotions can indifferently be directed at the past ('Ben regrets not having gone to the party'), the present ('Rosetta is embarrassed by her behavior') and the future ('Arthur hopes that the weather will hold up'). Certain types of emotions tend to be directed at one or another of these temporal determinations (this is especially true of the past, remorse and nostalgia being two examples of emotions always directed at the past), but most emotions can, it seems, be about events across the temporal spectrum. Hope can for instance be about past events as when Ben hopes that his letter arrived at its destination. Emotions directed at the past will typically be based on the subject's memories but may also have testimony as their cognitive base, emotions directed at the present are typically based on perception, and emotions directed at the future are often grounded in imagination-based expectations of the relevant event. But of course the content of the relevant cognitive bases and so the content of the emotion might not be temporally indexed at all, as when I enjoy imagining visiting Rome. Note furthermore that some emotions require that the subject believes certain things concerning their object ('Ben regrets not having gone to the party' requires that Ben believes that he did not go), whereas others require the absence of these beliefs ('Ben hopes that he will go to the party' implies that he is uncertain whether or not he will go). Certain emotional episodes ('Ben fears that Nina went to the party without him') depend on some measure of uncertainty concerning the occurrence of the events in question. The fact that emotions essentially involve cognitive bases will play a crucial role in assessing different accounts of what emotions are.

We have seen that the emotions are always directed at objects that are provided by their cognitive bases. To refer to these objects provided by the cognitive bases of emotions, we shall use the term of art '*particular objects*', without implying by this that our emotions are always about ordinary material objects – we can worry about the state of the environment or admire a theory. Now, acknowledging that emotions have particular objects may still not seem to provide an exhaustive characterization of the intentionality of emotions. Indeed, emotions do have intentional objects that are provided by their cognitive bases, but they also seem to represent these objects in a characteristic way. Suppose Jane is sad because England lost to Germany. It is right to say that her sadness concerns the result of the match, but it is fair to add that this result is, from Jane's perspective, a bad thing. Jane takes England's defeat to be a bad thing, whereas a supporter of Germany takes it to be a good thing. Not only does she take the result to be bad, she takes it to be bad in a specific way – not in a despicable way (she would have felt contempt), nor in an offending way (she would have felt anger), but in a sad way (for she feels sadness). Emotions – or so some philosophers and psychologists tend to believe – connect with specific kinds of *evaluations* that make up different kinds of emotions. As we shall have ample opportunity to observe, it is indeed illuminating to think of sadness as being connected to the evaluation of its object as a loss, of anger as connected to an evaluation of it as offensive, of fear as connected to the threatening, of admiration as connected to the beautiful, etc. This would make a lot of sense given that our susceptibility to feel emotions seems intimately connected with our tendency to make evaluative judgments. For instance, I may judge someone to be offensive as a result of the anger I feel towards him.

There seem to be, then, at least two central aspects to the intentionality of the emotions, one linked to the fact that they have particular objects provided by their bases, the other linked to the fact that they seem intimately connected to evaluations of these objects. A crucial theme of this book concerns how we should understand the relations between these two aspects of the intentionality of emotions and whether or not their intentionality can be illuminated by appealing to their phenomenology.

## Epistemology

These two aspects of the intentionality of the emotions allow us to consider and criticize them from a variety of different perspectives. First, and as a direct consequence of their being directed at particular objects and connected with types of evaluations, emotions are subject to *standards of correctness*. If Leonard is afraid of Fido, a friendly and docile dog, we would tell him that the dog poses no danger and would consider his fear inappropriate. Some such standards seem to apply to all the emotions, though perhaps not – as we shall shortly see – to all affective phenomena. In this respect, emotions are similar to many cognitive states such as beliefs and perceptual experiences. All these states have conditions of correctness, i.e. they have a content in the light of which it is possible to assess whether they fit the facts or not (e.g., Searle 1983). The fact that emotions are assessed as correct or incorrect depending on whether or not they fit the facts has prompted philosophers to talk about them as having the mind-to-world direction of fit – they aim, as it were, at representing the world as it is – and we shall see later in this chapter that this allows us to draw an informative contrast between the emotions and other psychological states.

Second, standards of correctness so conceived should be distinguished from *epistemological standards* by which we assess the justification of emotions.

Indeed, emotions are often assessed as justified or unjustified in light of the reasons the subject has for them. Bernard has good reasons to be elated if he has just heard from a reliable witness that his wife is in much better health. His reasons would be bad were his elation based on a report from a notoriously unreliable witness. In short, our emotions are sometimes justified, and sometimes unjustified. And they can be unjustified even if, by chance perhaps, they meet the standard of correctness just mentioned. That is the case if, although Bernard's wife is really in good health, his elation is based on the testimony of an unreliable informant. In this last respect, emotions resemble beliefs, for which we also often request reasons (that may or may not justify them), and differ from perceptions that can be said to be correct or incorrect but which are not justified by reasons. This also seems to constitute a sharp contrast between emotions and moods: we tend not to think of moods such as grumpiness as either correct or incorrect or as justified or unjustified.[2]

For now, let us stress that it is important not to confuse the standards of correctness and justification with still further standards which we also use to assess the emotions. Say Alison laughs at a funny joke told by Bernard, but Roger rebukes her by pointing out that the joke is cruel towards some of the people present. Let us imagine that the joke actually is funny, so Alison's amusement is still appropriate in the first sense outlined above: the emotion fits its object. Yet Alison's amusement is nonetheless inappropriate in a different way. The emotion falls short of another kind of standard, one of propriety or morality (D'Arms and Jacobson 2000). Or consider another case: René is completely desperate, he thinks he has no chances of passing his exam. Suppose in addition that he has every reason to feel that way: he knows the exam to be difficult, knows that he is very behind in his preparation, etc. In the light of these reasons, his emotion must be assessed as justified. Still, there is a sense in which it might be thought to be inappropriate. Indeed, from a prudential perspective, he would be better off without it.

We have noted the various perspectives from which emotions can be assessed. In chapters to come, we will revisit from various angles questions regarding the best way to understand the standards of correctness of emotions, and we will develop our account of them in Chapter 7. And, while issues relating to the standard of justification for emotions will constitute a recurring theme, the various epistemological issues surrounding the justification of emotions and their relations with evaluative judgments will be the focus of the last three chapters of this book.

## Emotions within the affective domain

We have introduced a number of distinctions that serve to highlight some differences between emotions and other psychological states, such as beliefs and perceptions on the one hand, and between them and other affective states such as moods on the other hand. Some of these same distinctions will now help us contrast the emotions with yet other psychological phenomena closely related to them, and that will be the center of many of the discussions to come. We shall first focus on affective dispositions, and then on desires.

Consider the following statement: 'Leonard is angry with Nina'. This statement, outside of any particular context, can be read in two different ways. On the one hand, it is possible to understand it as saying that Leonard is at this moment in the grip of anger. Here reference is being made to a particular *episode* of anger. But the statement can also be read, not as saying that Leonard is currently boiling with rage, but merely that he tends to feel anger towards Nina in certain circumstances, for instance, when he is in her presence. In this case, the statement refers to an *affective disposition* that Leonard has. As opposed to emotional episodes, it makes no sense to ask at what particular moment an affective disposition takes place. Given that attributions of emotions are almost universally subject to this kind of ambiguity, it is important to keep the distinction between episodes and dispositions in mind.[3] While we believe that ordinary language does not give us any reason to favor the episodic rather than the dispositional reading, it is clear that these two uses refer to very different phenomena. Observe also that in the foregoing we have reserved, in line with most contemporary research in both psychology and philosophy,[4] the term 'emotion' for the relevant affective episodes. This is of course not to imply that affective dispositions are irrelevant to the study of the emotions. On the contrary, it is very important to distinguish several kinds of affective dispositions and to understand the variety of relations they have with emotional episodes.

To this end, one distinction is of particular value. Affective dispositions can be 'single-track' – concerning a single emotion, or they can be 'multi-track' – concerning several emotions. So in the case of statements such as 'Leonard is angry at Nina' (on the dispositional reading) or 'Leonard is envious of the rich', we are attributing to him single-track dispositions (they concern, respectively, only anger and envy). Ordinary language does not have a term to refer specifically to this kind of disposition and, for lack of a better term, we shall henceforth refer to them as *emotional dispositions*.

Let us now consider multi-track dispositions. If Juliette loves Romeo, she is not just disposed to feel some specific emotion towards him (erotic ecstasy? warm affection? fawning admiration?), but also grief if things turn sour, pride at his accomplishments, or jealousy at the sight of a rival. The same structure can be found in hatred. Hating someone does not consist in being disposed to feel any single emotion but, among other things, to feel glee at the other's misfortune or indignation at the help he receives from third parties. Following one traditional use of this expression (e.g., Broad 1954: 212–14, Frijda 2007: 192–93), we shall call these types of affective dispositions '*sentiments*'.

There is also a third sort of disposition. Being kind-hearted, being honest, being insensitive, being frivolous are also multi-track dispositions, but, unlike sentiments, they do not seem to focus on any particular object but rather generally on any object insofar as it is apprehended in some particular evaluative light. The honest person will be concerned with how the value of honesty fares and the kind person will be especially sensitive to the disvalue of suffering. While they focus on values rather than on particular objects, the structure of these multi-track dispositions is similar to that of the sentiments in implying tendencies to experience some particular family of emotions (the kind person will have a greater than normal tendency to feel, say, pity, gratitude, and affection), or alternatively tendencies not to experience some array of emotions in some particular way (for instance, an inconsiderate person is someone who will be blind to occasions for emotions such as gratitude and compassion). These dispositions are, in everyday discourse, classed as *character traits*. We hasten to add that emotions are only one of the various manifestations of character traits and sentiments, which also find expression in one's actions and habits of thought. Equally, virtues and vices constitute only a subset of character traits, a subset comprising those traits that have to do to some degree with our moral or intellectual life.

These various affective dispositions are clearly intentional phenomena. Their intentionality will be a function of the intentionality of the emotions that manifest them, and their objects will differ depending on the type of affective disposition considered. They differ from emotions and moods as regards phenomenology, however. Affective dispositions have no felt quality, save derivatively through the emotions in which they find expression (if Leonard is angry with Nina – in the dispositional sense – he remains so even when his mind is entirely occupied with other matters). Finally, it is also probably correct to regard affective dispositions as properties of the individual, which in principle last longer than an emotion or a mood (Leonard's dispositional anger can last two weeks or a lifetime).

In Chapter 9, we shall provide a more detailed account of the nature of these various affective dispositions. For now, let us turn to desires, which are also often regarded as belonging to the affective domain. What are the differences, if any, between desires and emotions? Here are some salient features of desires that suggest that they differ in more than cosmetic detail from emotions.

First, some episodic desires are not felt, though violent or urgent desires will be. Contrast for instance your episodic desire to go to Spain next year, which may not feel any specific way, with your episodic desire to rush to the bathroom. Second, desires are not obviously episodic in nature, occurring at a given time, as emotions are. To say at a given time that you desire to go to Spain next year is not obviously to assert that you are at that time having a mental episode of desiring something, since the affirmation may be correct even when you are completely wrapped up in some unrelated activity or when you are asleep. Third, we have noted that emotions can, but need not, be attitudes directed towards states of affairs, as revealed by the fact that many verbs for emotions can indifferently take propositional or nominal complements. Desires, however, always appear to be attitudes towards states of affairs. There is indeed good reason to believe that when we make assertions such as 'Fred wants a gourmet dinner' or 'Maria wants Paul', these nominal constructions are ellipses for propositional constructions. One argument for this is as follows: it is always possible to add a temporal modifier to a desire attribution with a nominal content (for instance, 'Fred wants a gourmet dinner *before the end of the week*'), where the temporal modifier concerns what is desired and not the time at which the psychological state of desire takes place. That is to say, Fred *now* wants a certain state of affairs – i.e. that he enjoy a gourmet dinner at some time between now and Sunday.[5] Fourth, desires, in contrast to emotions, are always about states of affairs that the subject does not believe already obtain. If Sam believes that Mary died, he can be happy about it or regret it, but he cannot want her to die. Fifth, there is a colorable case that desires, being essentially motivational states (e.g., Hume 1975, Smith 1994), are internally related to the subject's conviction that she can, directly or indirectly, do something to bring about what she desires (or, more modestly, to the subject's lack of conviction that she cannot do anything to bring it about). While emotions also have important links with action, the link is much weaker, as shown by the case of emotions directed at the past. Sam might regret what he has done while fully aware that he cannot undo it in any way. In this connection, it is often pointed out that it would be odd, for example, to attribute to Sam a desire that some event had not occurred. Indeed, when the event lies in the past, we speak instead of Sam's wish that it had not occurred.

At this stage, it already looks like desires differ significantly from emotions. Unlike emotions, desires are not always felt and often seem to be dispositions rather than episodes. Their respective intentional features also display interesting disanalogies: desires appear to be essentially directed towards states of affairs that are not believed to obtain, and seem to exhibit an essential link with the subject's awareness of a possibility to act.

Nevertheless, this series of contrasts can seem superficial. After all, nothing in what has been said lets us make a fundamental distinction between felt desires and emotions such as hope, nor between wishes and emotions directed at the past. Does this mean that nothing ultimately distinguishes them? The difference between desires and other conative phenomena, on the one hand, and emotions, on the other hand, is arguably situated at a more fundamental level that also concerns their respective intentionality. This difference comes down to the fact that desires and emotions have opposite *directions of fit*. Indeed, conative phenomena like desires have a world-to-mind direction of fit (e.g., Searle 1983). That is to say, the point of a desire is to bring about changes in the world so that the world comes to be as it is represented by the desire. And when this happens, or (in a stronger version of the idea) when the desire of the agent causes an action that brings about these changes, the desire is satisfied or fulfilled. On this stronger interpretation, if Fred desires to invite Mary to the party, his desire is satisfied or fulfilled when he sends his invitation.

This feature does not seem to be shared by the other affective phenomena, in particular emotions. It does not seem to make sense to say of an episode of fear or sadness that it is 'fulfilled' in this sense. If what I feared would happen ends up happening, we won't say that my fear is satisfied or fulfilled (for it did not aim at being fulfilled in the way a desire with the same content would); rather, we would say that it turned out to be correct or justified. There was something right about being afraid that it would happen. To recall, we assess emotions rather along the same lines as the way we assess beliefs or perceptions: they are correct or incorrect depending on whether things actually stand (or stood or will stand) as they are represented by the belief or the perception. That is to say, emotions have the opposite – mind-to-world – direction of fit. Desires may of course still have correctness conditions (mind-to-world direction of fit) in addition to fulfillment conditions (world-to-mind direction of fit), but the fact that they have the latter sets them clearly apart from emotions and other affective phenomena.[6] However, this difference in directions of fit has not prevented a number of philosophers from defending the idea that emotions can be cashed out in terms of desires, or that they contain a certain desire as an essential part. In Chapter 3 we will revisit the issue of these mental states' directions of fit as well as the question of what role desires have, if any, in an account of the emotions. More generally, we shall have to explore the motivational role characteristic of emotions, a role which we suggested differs markedly from that of desires.

This completes our survey of the different affective states that we might want to distinguish from the emotions, i.e. moods, desires, character traits, sentiments, and affective dispositions generally. While differing from the emotions, all of these affective states are among their main determinants; we often appeal to them to explain why we respond emotionally in the way we do. Now, as already mentioned, one of the central issues of this book is the question of the conditions under which emotions are justified. It goes without saying, then, that an account of justified emotions will have to assess the potential epistemological roles played by all these affective states, something we shall do in Chapter 9.

## Conclusion

This first approach to the emotions has helped us picture them in the following way. Emotions are episodes that have a felt character and are directed at particular objects provided by their cognitive bases. They appear moreover to be intimately related to evaluations of these objects and are subject to assessment by means of a variety of distinct standards, most prominently among them standards of correctness and justification. We have also seen how the distinctions we introduced to picture the emotions in that way allow us to tell them apart from other psychological states in general and other affective states more particularly. While we believe that this rough portrayal of the emotions is essentially faithful to their nature, the journey we are about to embark on in the following pages will illustrate that none of the ideas it rests on should be naively accepted, for not one has gone unchallenged. As a matter of fact, the very idea that emotions constitute a respectable psychological category for philosophical or scientific inquiry has been seriously challenged, as we shall see in the next chapter.

## Questions and further readings

(1)   What are the different types of standards by means of which we assess emotions?
(2)   We said that emotions have cognitive bases. What is a cognitive base?
(3)   Is it possible to draw a principled distinction between emotions and desires?

We have alluded to the idea, without discussing it, that emotions are *passive* phenomena. That is, emotions, much like perceptions and in contrast to episodes of imagining, are not subject to the will. For a different point of view, see Sartre (1948) and Solomon (1973). For a very helpful discussion of the passivity of the emotions and its connections with the way we speak of them, see Gordon (1987).

Philosophers who have laid great emphasis on the *felt character* of the emotions in recent years are Pugmire (1998) and Stocker (1983). For a very wide-ranging review of the way feelings might be thought to be involved in the emotions, see Lambie and Marcel (2002).

On the topic of the *intentionality* of the emotions, de Sousa (1987) remains the best discussion, notably in the way it distinguishes the various senses in which emotions can be said to have objects (see in particular Chapter 5). For the idea that mental states in general and emotions in particular can have non-propositional objects, see Montague (2007).

Regarding the various *standards* to which the emotions are answerable or the different senses in which we may say that emotions are appropriate or inappropriate, see D'Arms and Jacobson (2000), Rabinowicz and Rønnow-Rasmussen (2004), and Tappolet (2011).

The classical discussion of the notion of directions of fit in general and its application to *desires* in particular is found in Searle (1983). For a helpful discussion of this notion, see Humberstone (1992). Schroeder (2004: Chapter 1) offers a very useful survey of contemporary approaches to the nature of desires. The widespread thesis that desires are essentially motivational states is convincingly defended (against Schroeder amongst others) in Wall (2009).

We have suggested that *moods* differ from emotions in that they are not subject to standards of correctness, a topic we shall develop in Chapter 9. For three different views that nevertheless converge on the idea that moods are closer to the emotions than we suggest, see Crane (1998), Goldie (2000: Chapter 6), and Prinz (2004: Chapter 8). For an important and very different approach to the topic of moods in the contemporary literature, see Ratcliffe (2008). For a general survey of affective dispositions, see Ben Ze'ev (2000: Chap. 4).

## Notes

1   The discussion here alludes to the question of whether emotions, or some emotions, exhibit, like perceptions for example, a feature philosophers refer to as 'factivity'. For a defense of the factivity of certain emotions, see Gordon (1987) and, for a critique of this view, Wollheim (1999: 103–10).

2 According to an alternative and widespread view, moods are evaluative apprehensions of 'the whole world' or some vaguely specified aspects of it. While not deprived of intuitive plausibility – it might be one way of affirming that moods color our experience – we believe that this view should be given up since it implies that moods should almost always be assessed as incorrect and unjustified, rather than being not subject to the relevant standards. See also the 'Questions and further readings' section and Chapter 9, pp. 105–106.

3 For a discussion of the distinction between dispositions and occurrences in the affective domain, see Lyons (1980: 53–57) and Mulligan (1998).

4 Two important exceptions are Goldie (2000) and Wollheim (1999).

5 This argument is presented in Searle (1983: 30). For discussion and further references, see Montague (2007: 508).

6 The fact that beliefs aim at adjusting themselves to the way the world is has led some (e.g., Searle 1983: Chapter 1) to think of them as satisfied when they succeed in adjusting themselves in that way. Satisfaction in this sense is obviously not what we mean when we speak of fulfillment in connection with desires, since beliefs never aim at adjusting the world to how they represent it. The fact that, unlike desires, beliefs or emotions do not aim at being fulfilled is brought to light when we consider the impact of evidence that their respective contents do not obtain. Other things being equal, one ceases to believe that it is raining when confronted with evidence that it is not raining, one ceases to fear getting attacked by the lion when one sees that its cage is locked, but one continues to desire to solve the puzzle when confronted with evidence that one has not solved it yet.

# 2   The diversity and unity of emotions

In the previous chapter, we highlighted the diversity of the affective domain by drawing attention to some important differences between the emotions and other affective phenomena. In the present chapter, we turn to an examination of the diversity within the category of emotion. We shall inquire whether there are important differences amongst the phenomena that we call emotions, and, if so, whether this casts doubts on the fundamental unity of this category. To do so, we have to examine more closely some of the important distinctions that can be made within the narrower domain of emotions. We shall start by considering some distinctions, primarily those between positive and negative emotions and between conscious and unconscious emotions, contrasts within the domain that in our opinion do not threaten the unity of the category as a whole. Next, we shall turn our attention to another distinction, that between basic and nonbasic emotions, which structures many current debates about the emotions. Since it has been argued that this distinction puts into question the unity and theoretical interest of the common-sense category of emotion, our discussion culminates with an evaluation of this suggestion.

## Positive and negative emotions

A first distinction that structures our intuitive grasp of the emotional domain is that between positive and negative emotions. Intuitively, sadness, fear, disgust, shame, and regret count as negative, while joy, admiration, pride, and amusement count as positive. In this context philosophers and psychologists speak of the 'polarity' or 'valence' of emotions. Accounting for this central aspect of emotional phenomena has typically taken one of two forms: we may approach valence in hedonic or in conative terms.

The hedonic approach has it that the various kinds of emotions are to be classed as positive or negative in virtue of 'what it is like' to experience them. The idea here, one that already surfaced in our brief discussion of the phenomenology of the emotions in Chapter 1, is that each kind of emotion is among other things essentially a kind of pleasure or displeasure, pleasure and displeasure being considered as irreducible, phenomenological qualities (hence the talk in terms of the positive or negative hedonic quality of an emotion). This is perfectly compatible with the idea that certain kinds of emotions are hedonically ambivalent (e.g., nostalgia and scorn). A strong version of this view would then consist in claiming that each emotion-*type* essentially possesses a certain hedonic quality, i.e. it is either positive, negative, or mixed.

The case of surprise, however, poses a problem for this strong variant of the thesis: there are positive surprises, just as there are negative surprises. A weaker version of the view might then hold that every particular emotional *episode* essentially has a certain hedonic quality. Is this modest claim more persuasive? Once again, surprise looks like an exception: some episodes of surprise are hedonically neutral. And hedonic neutrality is not a hedonic quality as such, it is just the absence of any hedonic quality.

However one chooses to respond to the peculiar problem of surprise, be it by admitting the existence of an exception to these claims or by refusing – precisely on the grounds of its exceptional nature – to consider hedonically neutral episodes of surprise as genuine emotions, we may nevertheless think that the viability of the hedonic quality conception of valence will not turn on its ability to account for the single and admittedly quite peripheral case of surprise. Indeed, this conception faces a much more serious difficulty: when we turn our attention to the phenomenology of many emotions – think of anger or pity for instance – it is not clear at all that they are, even in part, pleasures or displeasures. While joy and sadness may perhaps be understood as involving a certain hedonic quality akin to what we encounter in cases of bodily pleasures and pains, nothing of the sort appears to be true of the examples just presented. This problem, not to mention the fact that the very idea of pleasures and displeasures as intrinsic properties of experiences has been the target of many recent criticisms (e.g., Clark 2005), has led many to favor the second natural way of understanding valence, an approach predicated on the idea that emotions are essentially motivational states.

This alternative approach to valence in conative terms has taken at least three forms. One can cash out the contrast between positive and negative emotions in terms of (a) motivational tendencies, where positive emotions are those that involve attraction to the object of the emotion, and negative emotions feature a kind of aversion towards it (e.g., McLean 1993), or in terms of (b) desires concerning the mental state in which one finds oneself (in positive emotions, the subject wants the intentional state she is in to continue, and in negative emotions she wants it to stop) (e.g., Prinz 2004: 173–74), or in terms of (c) frustration or satisfaction of desires (positive emotions are those that reveal to her that a given situation is congruent with [some of] her goals, and negative emotions reveal an incongruence) (e.g., Lazarus 1991).

These alternative theories seem no less problematic than the one in terms of hedonic qualities outlined above. We shall be in a position to weigh their merits only at a later stage of our discussion, when we will have gained a better understanding of the connections between emotions and desires, a connection that, as already mentioned, takes center stage in many theories of the emotions. With our conclusions regarding these connections in hand and in the light of our own theory of the emotions in Chapter 7, we shall suggest that there is no reason to think that the kind of intuitions we have about the positive or negative character of the emotions are answerable to any one monochrome conative or hedonic feature of the emotions.

## Conscious and unconscious emotions

Another objection to the hedonic approach to valence we have not yet mentioned appeals to the contrast between conscious and unconscious emotions. If there are such things as unconscious emotions, then it hardly makes sense to conceive of the positive and negative aspects of emotions in terms of pleasures and pains understood as irreducible phenomenological qualities. Indeed, it is quite difficult to understand the claim that phenomenological qualities of this sort may occur below the threshold of consciousness when we undergo unconscious emotions.

This line of thought appeals to the important distinction between conscious and unconscious emotions, a distinction that is the object of vigorous debate in the literature. Why think unconscious emotions exist at all if, as we have implied in Chapter 1, emotions are essentially felt? Three main considerations can be adduced in favor of this claim. First of all, Freud has accustomed us to regarding a significant portion of our behavior as derived from unconscious motivations, amongst which many are affective in nature. It is for instance Charles's repressed – and hence unconscious – guilt concerning his first daughter's premature death that explains his tendency to spoil his other children. The same applies to his hatred towards his mother, a sentiment he discovers only after years of psychoanalysis. Second, it seems that some emotions, just like some pains, are not felt. I injure myself during a race but only feel the pain after I cross the finish line. Similarly, I only become conscious of my anger when Bernard points out that I have been behaving atrociously for the last few minutes. Third, when psychologists have established a correlation between the activation of certain nervous centers and subjects reporting that they feel a given emotion, they sometimes conclude that an unconscious emotion is present in cases where a similar activation is observed in the absence of the usual subject self-report.

Although these considerations point to real and important phenomena, they do not seem to us to threaten the idea that emotions are essentially felt. It is noteworthy that the term 'unconscious' covers several distinct kinds of phenomena: (a) something may be called unconscious merely in virtue of the fact that one's attention is not at the present time directed towards it. As you concentrate on the lines of this text, you are in this sense now not conscious of the feel of your clothes on your body. This does not mean that you are not sensing your clothes' texture, tightness, rubbing motion, and the like. The above example of Bernard making me aware of my anger is a clear illustration of this use of 'unconscious': I was angry, I was experiencing all the things that make up what it is like for me to be angry, but my attention was simply focused elsewhere (see Goldie 2000: 62–72). If Bernard had not remarked on it, I might never have become conscious of it in this sense. We can deal in a similar fashion with the many cases where a certain neuronal activity is observed in a subject who does not report the experience of any emotion. The fact that she does not report experiencing or having experienced the emotion might be more a reflection of her attention being focused elsewhere than a sign that she did not feel the emotion.

An emotion may also be called 'unconscious' (b) insofar as the subject has never viewed it as falling under a certain concept. When we attribute to Charles an unconscious guilt, as in the example above, we may mean that he has never conceived of some of the various feelings the death of his daughter arouses in him as episodes of guilt. Now, this very fact might lend itself to a variety of explanations. Charles might simply not have given any thought to the nature of these feelings, or perhaps he has and has misidentified them (he may even fail to realize that they are part of an emotion), or perhaps he is in one way or another engaged in self-deception about what he feels. But none of these explanations presuppose or motivate the idea that he did not feel guilt. In connection with this sense of the term 'unconscious', note that the length and difficulty of the process of conceptualizing one's emotions can vary greatly. For instance, all things being equal, it is more difficult to properly identify emotions felt in the distant past than more recent emotions, and more difficult to do so with some emotion types than others. This is why coming to a verdict sometimes requires serious deliberation or perhaps even therapy.

Finally, it is also worth mentioning that other cases we are inclined to think of as unconscious may well be best conceived of (c) in terms of some of the affective *dispositions* we introduced in Chapter 1. So, for instance, Charles's hatred for his mother can be understood in terms of the existence of a multi-track disposition centered on her: Charles gets irritated in her presence, systematically makes derogatory remarks about her, tries his best to avoid meeting her, and so on. His hatred in this case is not an unconscious emotion, for it is not an emotion at all. As with the first two senses of 'unconscious', then, it appears that nothing here threatens the general thesis according to which emotions are felt: the emotions that manifest this disposition are (or have in the past been) felt.

But may one not insist that emotions can be unconscious in a yet stronger sense? Are we not ready to say that some emotions can be unconscious in the sense that the subject never felt them? An affirmative answer amounts to saying in Charles's case that he was overcome with guilt because of the death of his daughter despite never having felt the weight of wrongdoing with regard to it. Only on this interpretation of the term 'unconscious' does the claim that unconscious emotions exist pose a real threat to the idea that emotions are essentially felt. That being said, all the sorts of cases mentioned above are perfectly intelligible without any need to posit such a strong form of unconsciousness, which has the additional handicap of running up against the common-sense intuition that there always is something it is like to undergo an emotion.

In conclusion, we can say that there is no inconsistency in both asserting that unconscious emotions exist, in various senses of this expression, and holding onto the idea that emotions are essentially felt.

## Other distinctions

We want now to briefly mention three other distinctions often discussed in the literature. First, there is the distinction between reflexive and non-reflexive emotions. In the former class we find emotions such as guilt, shame, pride, embarrassment, and the like. The idea here is that these emotions are distinctive in virtue of the fact that the subject has an attitude towards herself when undergoing the emotion. Feeling shame at one's misdeed, say, requires thinking of this misdeed as reflecting negatively upon oneself; and it is because one perceives a specific connection between a given achievement and oneself that it elicits pride rather than mere joy or envy, for example.

Another distinction is between first-order and second-order emotions. While most emotions are directed at worldly events, objects or processes, emotions can also be directed at other mental states, including other emotions. A second-order emotion is then an emotion directed at another emotion, as when you are ashamed of your fear, or when you are proud of feeling indignation. Second-order emotions are often thought to play an important role in the way we assess and regulate our first-order emotional responses. Your disappointment regarding the anger you felt at being confronted with your wrongdoing might be the beginning of an assessment of your anger as inappropriate and an attempt at self-reform.

And finally, a class of moral emotions is often distinguished from non-moral emotions. Compassion, guilt, and indignation are often cited as examples of the moral sort, because of the central role they play in the apprehension of situations relevant to morality, or because they inherently have a moral value (compassion being for instance conceived of as morally good and envy as morally bad).

These three distinctions testify to the richness and complexity of our emotional lives. Self-reflexive emotions allow us to affectively react to some events because we are distinctively implicated in them and constitute a distinctive type of affective self-consciousness. Second-order emotions, we have seen, may prove very important in connection with our capacity to regulate our own emotional lives. And, needless to say, investigating the nature and roles of moral emotions is indispensible in order to understand how our moral concerns may become affectively manifest (think for instance of the connections between emotions, virtues, and vices), and also to appreciate the roles and nature of moral judgments.

## Basic emotions

The distinctions that we have sought to clarify in the last sections share two features. They are distinctions made within the domain of emotions without questioning in any way the unity of this category, and they propose no ordering in terms of priority of any kind within the domain. This is not true of the last distinction, which remains to be elucidated and which plays a fundamental role in the recent literature: the distinction between basic and nonbasic emotions. The idea consists in applying straightforwardly to the domain of emotions the model that has met with great success in other fields of research: complex observed phenomena are seen as the outcome of a limited set of basic building blocks with which more complex phenomena are constructed. Think of the elements of the periodic table, which constitute the basic building blocks of chemical molecules. Why apply such a model to the domain of emotions? Intuitively, certain emotions appear more complex than others. For instance, nostalgia seems more complex than regret, and regret more complex than fear. This intuition finds expression for example in the fact that we have no difficulty in attributing certain emotions to animals (e.g., fear or joy) but we balk at endowing them with others (e.g., regret, hope). Are these pre-theoretical intuitions warranted?

The idea that we should distinguish basic elements from derivative elements within the domain of emotions is of course not new. The Stoics recognized four basic emotions: delight, distress, desire, and fear (see Graver 2007). Hobbes allowed for seven 'simple passions': appetite, desire, love, aversion, hatred, joy, and grief (1668/1994: I, Chapter 6), whereas Descartes suggested a somewhat different list: admiration-surprise, love, hate, desire, joy, and sadness (1649/1989: Part 2). Thus the ambition to define all the emotions in terms of a set of basic emotions has a long history, although the pretenders to the title of 'basic emotion' have varied greatly from one theory to the next. Moreover, many of the proposed analyses suggested by these authors are far from convincing. Should we, for instance, countenance Hobbes's claim that fear is nothing other than an aversion for an object that you believe will affect you?

Whatever specific difficulties each of these classic theories may face, the general idea that there exists a fundamental distinction between basic and nonbasic emotions is still central to recent discussions, principally thanks to the influence of Darwin. The psychologist Paul Ekman has played an important role in developing this idea (e.g., Ekman 1972). His understanding of the distinction amounts to counting as 'basic' all those emotions that are universally shared. On Ekman's account, universality is measured through the recognition of facial expressions across different cultures, a method pioneered by Darwin (1872/1998). Others have linked the universal character of basic emotions to the fact that they have a traceable evolutionary history because they proved helpful in meeting distinct environmental challenges for our ancestors (e.g., Cosmides and Tooby 2000, Plutchik 1980), or to the fact that they have a correlate and distinct neural pathway (e.g., Panksepp 2000). These three criteria are not only mutually compatible, but on the present approaches they should converge. This is why we today speak of basic emotions or 'affect programs' in all cases where emotional episodes correspond to a profile involving changes of a systematic kind across the following dimensions:

- changes in facial expression of the emotion;
- muscular changes (in orientation, posture);
- expressive vocal changes;
- changes in the hormonal system;
- changes in the nervous system.

Closely associated to this school of thought, one finds the idea that the systems responsible for these changes are to a large extent *modular* in Fodor's sense (1983), i.e. among other things that they are (i) automatic, (ii) specific to a restricted domain of stimuli, (iii) quick, and (iv) cognitively impenetrable. To illustrate, consider fear. The systems responsible for fear responses are automatic because the subject has no direct control over them (this echoing the passivity of emotions alluded to in Chapter 1); they take a restricted domain of stimuli as input because the range of things that elicit fear is quite limited; they are quick in the sense that the processing of these stimuli elicits the fear response almost instantaneously; and they are cognitively impenetrable because they function independently of the other cognitive states the subject may happen to have (for example, a moving snake will typically elicit fear even if one believes it is harmless).

At this stage, it is important to emphasize that the criterion by which basic emotions are distinguished from nonbasic emotions in contemporary psychology is very specific, and in all likelihood very different from that employed in the classical philosophical theories. For contemporary theorists an emotion counts as basic if it satisfies the general profile just sketched. Basic emotions are not states that result from a learning process. In other words, they are innate responses (Prinz 2004). Yet, even on this single criterion, it does not seem easy to come up with a definitive answer as to which emotions are basic: there is surprisingly little agreement among the various lists of basic emotions generated by applying the notion of affect program. The first list proposed by Ekman included only six emotions: surprise, fear, anger, disgust, sadness, and joy. The most recent version includes 15, among which we find emotions that appear much more sophisticated such as shame and guilt (Ekman 1997). Beyond the fact that research in many of the relevant fields is only in its infancy, this state of affairs can be explained in part by the seeming lack of convergence between the different criteria put forward by emotion scientists. After all, it is not obvious that whenever an emotion is associated with a distinct facial expression, it also has a dedicated neural circuitry and a specific adaptive function, or vice versa (Roberts 2003: 14–36).

## Emotions: unity or diversity?

Even if we assume that such a convergence does exist, the distinction between basic and nonbasic emotions still requires that we answer two further questions.

First, does the word 'emotion', as an umbrella term covering both kinds of state, correspond to a coherent and unified class of mental states? Second, and directly related to this, how are we to understand the relation between these two kinds of emotions? We consider each of these questions in turn.

Linguistic considerations may make one hesitate to answer the first question in the affirmative. The word 'emotion' has no universal translation, far from it. In fact it is relatively recent (see Dixon 2003). In the past, one spoke of 'passions', a word that did apply to what we now call emotions, but also to pleasure, pain, and desire. It is also difficult to find words that are exactly equivalent to 'emotion' in other contemporary languages. Moreover, it may seem that this class of mental phenomena is more problematic than others, such as belief, perception, or memory. For one thing, we have no similarly elaborate classification of beliefs or perceptions; we distinguish beliefs or perceptions primarily by means of their specific contents (in the case of beliefs, a proposition). By contrast, in the case of emotions we have numerous sub-classes (hope, fear, horror, etc.) that we do not distinguish by means of their contents or at least not solely in this way. For instance, one may hope, fear, be horrified, that there will be rain. In light of these considerations, one might incline towards the conclusion that emotions are not likely to form a distinct and coherent class of phenomena.

The distinction between basic and nonbasic emotions has itself recently been used to deny the unity of the class of emotion. How so? We have already noted that basic emotions could be regarded as 'affect programs'. And affect programs look like *natural kinds*, since their similar surface properties seem to derive from the workings of the same underlying mechanisms. If this is so, we need only wait patiently for affective science to divulge the true number and nature of these affect programs. However, since it is not easy to elucidate all the phenomena that we refer to by 'emotion' in terms of affect programs and their properties, we may be tempted to think that the class contains phenomena that have little in common. That is to say, there may be reasons to consider the predicament we find ourselves in when we use the term 'emotion' as comparable to our use of the term 'jade'. We use the latter for both jadeite and nephrite compounds due to their surface properties – i.e. their similarity in perceptual appearance – although they constitute two distinct natural kinds of minerals with different molecular structures.

This is precisely the position defended by Griffiths (1997), who in an influential study focuses on the alleged lack of scientific rigor in the category *emotion*. In his view, a category of phenomena is a respectable candidate for scientific investigation only if it constitutes a natural kind, since only natural kinds are such as to permit 'rich collections of generalizations' about the phenomena belonging to them. This is so because natural kinds are sets of things that share similar surface properties in virtue of the workings of similar or identical underlying causal mechanisms. But when the similarity of surface properties is not due to the existence of similar underlying causal mechanisms, as in the case of jadeite and nephrite, there is no rich collection of generalizations and so the relevant classes of phenomena are not interesting candidates for scientific investigation. And, according to Griffiths, the various phenomena we call 'emotions' carve out a category that is in this respect similar to that carved out by our use of the term 'jade': in that case too, the similarity in surface properties – which explains why we have conceived of this category in the first place – cannot be explained through the workings of similar underlying causal mechanisms. Amongst the phenomena we call 'emotions', those that qualify as affect programs constitute a respectable category from a scientific point of view, but those that do not qualify require very different causal explanations and must for that reason be reclassified in quite distinct psychological categories. As a result, the concept of emotion is to be abandoned, and replaced by a new taxonomy of the relevant domain.

On Griffiths's account, our common-sense concept of emotion is applied not only to affect programs, but also to two other kinds of psychological phenomena, which he calls, respectively, 'irruptive motivations' and 'disclaimed actions' (Griffiths 1997: Chapters 5 and 6). The category of 'irruptive motivations' contains states that are cognitively more sophisticated than affect programs. An example of irruptive motivation is Helen's guilt for not attending Luke's talk. Although they share certain traits with affect programs, they differ insofar as they require of the subject a mastery and exercise of complex concepts (guilt arguably depends on the mastery of moral concepts, such as the concepts of responsibility and of wrongdoing), they do not constitute direct responses to challenges presented by the subject's immediate environment (is there a sort of challenge to which guilt directly responds?), and they can occur without any expressive or autonomic alterations (guilt appears to have neither a typical facial expression nor typical bodily manifestations), unlike affect programs such as fear or anger. 'Disclaimed actions' constitute a more problematic category: it includes the cases in which, for purposes of communication, we display the exterior signs of an emotion without feeling it (Mary's display of outrage at Luke's dirty joke). Should we go along with Griffiths's conclusion that the diversity of phenomena falling under the common-sense concept of emotion warrants rejecting the unity of the category?

No. Two strategies are available to defend the unity of this category. The first is to concede that Griffiths's conclusion is perhaps valid insofar as the interests of a certain science are concerned, while denying that these interests provide the only standard by which to judge whether any given category is worth serious investigation. After all, our classificatory practices do not have as their exclusive aim to correspond to natural kinds understood in the way sketched above. For instance, we classify many things on the basis of their functions – think for instance of the categories *watch*, *thermometer*, or *chair* – even though they do not have the relevant function in virtue of sharing similar or identical causal mechanisms – analogical, digital, and atomic watches for instance keep time thanks to completely different causal mechanisms.

In the same vein, understanding and explaining the thoughts, actions, and feelings of others may require the introduction of categories that do not correspond to natural kinds but nonetheless allow for interesting and perhaps practically indispensible collections of generalizations. This fact in itself might be reason enough to conclude that these categories are worth investigating (Goldie 2000: 103). Even if such a response might be appropriate in many other cases, it concedes too much to Griffiths as regards the category *emotion*. Indeed, the arguments he puts forward actually do not bear out his conclusion that the concept of emotion lacks a certain causal unity. This is precisely the flaw that the second strategy seeks to exploit.

As others have stressed (e.g., Roberts 2003: 14–36, Prinz 2004: 81–86), Griffiths has difficulty in showing that the categories of affect program and irruptive motivation are fundamentally distinct. Concerning disclaimed actions, Griffiths is indeed right in claiming that they do not belong with affect programs and irruptive motivations. But this fact does nothing to show that the category of emotion lacks unity, for it is quite unclear that the relevant phenomena even count as emotions in any ordinary sense. The fact that we can exploit our knowledge of the external displays of an emotion in order to achieve a certain communicative end (so that others will think that we feel the relevant emotion) only shows that we attribute emotions on the basis of signs that are not conclusive and can be manipulated. It in no way shows that disclaimed actions are part of what we conceive of as emotions.

The category of irruptive motivations is, however, not so easily disposed of, since irruptive motivations such as guilt are clearly amongst the phenomena covered by the category *emotion*. Since the crucial difference between irruptive motivations and affect programs consists in the fact that sophisticated cognitive capacities play a distinctive role in the former, the crux of the problem consists in evaluating whether the fact that such cognitive capacities are exercised supports the claim that irruptive motivations are not to be studied together with affect programs. This problem connects with an important and general issue we have to confront in order to understand the emotional domain. Note that sophisticated cognitive capacities can play a distinctive role with regard to all emotion types, and not only with regard to types of emotions such as guilt that we intuitively regard as more complex than others. Fear can for instance be triggered by quite complex thoughts, such as the belief that the stock market will crash. How do we account for this phenomenon? Should we conclude with Griffiths that such cases of 'fear' have nothing to do with the fear reaction triggered by the perception of a snake – a prototypical example of an affect program?

In grappling with these questions, it will be instructive to reconsider how affect programs and the affective phenomena dependent on higher cognitive processes might relate to each other. As we shall shortly see, a closer study of the relations between higher cognitive processes and affect programs, far from revealing an unbridgeable gap between them, will on the contrary allow us to make a distinction between basic and nonbasic emotions that is required on independent grounds anyway.

## Unity regained

To do so, let us look at two ways of understanding the relations between basic and nonbasic emotions. First, we can understand the latter as mixtures of basic emotions (Plutchik 2001). To mention just one example, nostalgia might be conceived of as a blend of joy and sadness. However, it is hard to apply this model to all emotions. Which basic emotions go to make up, say, reverence or envy? Moreover, even if this model can be so applied, it does not explain why non-human animals are incapable of having certain emotions: if they can feel joy and sadness, why can they not feel nostalgia? Why do these emotions not 'blend' in non-human animals? These difficulties both derive from a central flaw in this strategy: it does not take into account the complex cognitive states that play a role in many emotions.

The second more widespread option consists precisely in understanding nonbasic emotions as the product of interaction between basic emotions and cognitive states such as thoughts or beliefs. The most sophisticated version of this idea – which may amount to an elaboration of what some of the classic philosophers we mentioned had in mind – is formulated in terms of a 'calibration' of basic emotions mediated by these various cognitive states (Prinz 2004: 147–50). Affect programs are triggered automatically by specific kinds of stimuli, yet as the subject develops, these same affect programs come to be triggered by cognitive states. Certain combinations of cognitive states and affect programs triggered in this way are sufficiently important to receive their own label. Thus, for instance, 'jealousy' might be the name we give to anger when it is triggered by the belief that the affections of one's partner are directed at a third party; 'shame' might be the name we give to disgust when it is triggered by the belief that one has failed in some important way; and 'regret' the name of sadness triggered by an act performed in the past that is not reparable.

On this theory, a nonbasic emotion is nothing but a basic emotion caused by a judgment concerning a kind of circumstance that is seen as sufficiently important to receive a distinct name. In short, nonbasic emotions are nothing but basic emotions caused by certain sophisticated judgments, and their objects are merely a subset of the possible objects of basic emotions. So, for instance, in a world where the fate of the stock market became even more central to our lives than it is today, fear concerning market moves would receive its own name and would become a new kind of emotion, a nonbasic emotion. This explanatory framework strikes us as very promising. It is particularly convincing for example to consider indignation as a kind of anger caused by certain kinds of offending objects – those of a moral nature. Likewise, *Schadenfreude* may well be a form of joy caused by a kind of pleasing object – those pertaining to the misfortune of disliked others.

While it works for the two examples just given, this strategy cannot, however, be easily applied across the board. To be successful as a general strategy, there must be an analysis of this sort available for every nonbasic emotion. And, if the distinction between basic and nonbasic emotions is the same as that between affect programs and irruptive motivations (i.e. between emotions that depend on higher cognition and those that do not), the strategy is ill-advised. For, insofar as it can appeal to only a very restricted number of basic emotions, that is, those affective states that fulfill the very stringent conditions for qualifying as an affect program, it produces some rather unconvincing analyses; are, say, jealousy and shame really as suggested above nothing but kinds of anger and disgust?

We now see that neither of the possible ways of fleshing out the relationship between basic and nonbasic emotions can plausibly be regarded as applicable to the totality of the domain of emotions. Does this then mean that Griffiths's conclusion concerning the disunity of this domain stands? It does so only if the three distinctions – (i) between affect programs and irruptive motivations, (ii) between what is independent of higher cognitive states and what depends on them, and (iii) between phenomena that share surface properties in virtue of underlying causal mechanisms and those that do not – are in fact co-extensive. In particular, is it true that emotions that depend on higher cognitive states differ radically from affect programs?

One cannot exclude the possibility, for example, that instances of an emotion dependent on a certain complex judgment share similar underlying causal mechanisms, and therefore qualify as affect programs insofar as they implicate all the physiological and neural changes characteristic of them. For instance, if shame depends on complex evaluative judgments, as one might reasonably claim, and we were to discover that the expressive, physiological, and behavioral manifestations of shame were subtended by a specific underlying causal mechanism, there would be no reason, *pace* Griffiths, to not consider it an affect program. If for these reasons the true number of affect programs and thus the number of basic emotions were found to be considerably higher than previously thought (since being mediated by sophisticated cognitive states would not constitute a disqualifying trait), then the strategy of 'calibration' would only need to be employed in the cases where it seems plausible, as is the case for indignation and *Schadenfreude*. Now, while it is still an open empirical question how many distinct profiles of systematic patterns of change across the relevant neuronal and physiological dimensions there are underlying our emotional repertoire and to what extent they correspond to the way ordinary language carves the emotional domain,[1] the evidence leaves room for optimism (Aue and Scherer 2008, Charland 2002, Scherer 2009). If so, the reservations we raised regarding the calibration strategy can be retracted.

Now, of course, it is doubtful that Griffiths would be ready to countenance such a possibility. For, remember, affect programs are first and foremost characterized by their modularity, in particular by the fact that they are elicited by a restricted class of stimuli and are cognitively impenetrable. Affect programs obtain their naturalistic credentials from being directly responsive to a class of triggers that can be identified independently of the manner in which the subject assesses the relevance of these stimuli for his or her goals. In response, the following points should be raised. First, the very existence of well-defined classes of stimuli for any given type of emotion is in itself questionable. Trotting out the shopworn examples of snakes and spiders to delineate the class of stimuli relevant in the case of the fear affect program is often the best we can do in deploying this strategy. Many readers of Griffiths have indeed pointed out that his conclusion severs the natural continuity we find between the alleged automatic and more or less universal episodes of fear (e.g., at the sight of a spider) and the more sophisticated and idiosyncratic episodes of fear (e.g., at the consequences of having forgotten one's wallet on the plane). What this suggests is that it is probably a mistake to view any kind of emotional response as being in principle completely insulated from the influence of higher cognitive capacities.

Second, whatever one makes of these considerations, this strong modularity claim is not warranted by what may be perceived as the main motivation for Griffiths's view, i.e. the idea that affect programs play a crucial role in generating discriminative behavior in virtue of their being adaptive systematic responses to distinctive kinds of stimuli. The fact that the responses in question might sometimes be mediated by more complex cognitive states does not constitute in any way a threat to the idea that emotions systematically mediate between certain situations in the subject's environment and his or her behavioral responses. Of course, the soundness of this answer depends on the possibility of specifying what the relevant situations have in common, so as to account for the unity amongst the diverse and variously cognitively demanding instances of a given emotion type. What this commonality may amount to and how it relates to the subject's assessment of the circumstances in which she finds herself is something we shall discuss later (see Chapter 4). For now, let us conclude that there is good reason to think that, though the affective domain as a whole does contain phenomena of quite diverse natures, this is not true of the quite unified category of emotion.

## Conclusion

In this chapter, we have reviewed some important distinctions within the emotional domain. After having considered the distinctions between positive and negative emotions and between conscious and unconscious emotions, distinctions that do not threaten the unity of the category *emotion*, we have investigated the distinction between basic and nonbasic emotions. While some have appealed to this distinction in support of the thesis that this category exhibits no interesting unity, we have argued that there are reasons to resist this view. In particular, we have seen that the idea that there exists a class of emotions completely insulated from complex cognitive states is mistaken, and that there are no conclusive reasons for thinking that an emotion cannot belong to our basic emotional repertoire simply because it depends on such complex cognitive states.

## Questions and further readings

(1)  In what senses can there be unconscious emotions?
(2)  What are two common strategies for building complex emotions out of basic ones?
(3)  Why does Griffiths's argument about the disunity of the category *emotion* only go through if three distinctions – affect programs vs. irruptive motivations, cognitive independence vs. dependence, and natural kinds vs. other categories – converge?

Regarding *valence*, a good survey of the various theories is to be found in Colombetti (2005). A helpful recent reference is Prinz (2010). For skepticism about the idea that valence represents a unified phenomenon, see Cochrane (2009) and Solomon (2003).

A good discussion of the multifarious senses of the term 'unconscious' is to be found in Dainton (2000: Chapter 2). Two good recent discussions of the contrast between *conscious and unconscious emotions* are Hatzimoysis (2007) and Lacewing (2007). See also Greenspan (1988: Chapter 2), and, on this issue from an empirical perspective, Feldmann Barrett, Niedenthal and Winkielman (2005).

For a useful collection of studies on *reflexive emotions*, see Tracy, Robins and Tangney (2007). For an emphasis on the significance of negative reflexive emotions, see Deonna, Rodogno and Teroni (2011). On *second-order emotions*, see Jäger and Bartsch (2006) and, for their roles in emotion regulation, Gross (2007). A good starting point for the *moral emotions* is Rawls (1971). Williams (1973: Chapter 13) is very interesting but at times hard going. For empirically informed approaches to the moral emotions, see Haidt (2003) and Nichols (2004).

For a recent and nuanced defense of *basic emotions*, see Ekman (1997 and 2003). For skeptical takes on the usefulness of the category of basic emotions, see Solomon (2001) and Scherer and Ellgring (2007). On the many issues raised by the idea that emotions are modular, see the various contributions in Faucher and Tappolet (2006). For interesting reflexions on the philosophical significance of the way the emotions are treated in the sciences, see Pugmire (2006).

In addition to Roberts (2003: 14–36) and Prinz (2004: 81–86), who provide very good responses to Griffiths's skeptical challenge regarding *emotion as a category*, see Charland (2002).

## Note

1  The possibility that some terms for emotions as they feature in ordinary languages (e.g., 'fear') do not designate one basic emotion, but distinct ones (anxiety and fright, say) sharing some important similarities is discussed in Prinz (2004: Chapter 6).

# 3    Emotions, beliefs, and desires

The two first chapters dealt with some important traits of the emotions, distinguished emotions from other affective states, and examined some important distinctions within the emotional domain. Yet the task of understanding what emotions are still lies ahead of us. Remember that in the course of our discussion of basic and nonbasic emotions in the previous chapter we emphasized the important role of cognitive states, such as beliefs, while defending the unity of the category of emotion. In this chapter, we shall discuss in more detail the nature of the relationship between emotion and other cognitive states. This discussion will allow us to introduce and assess a first group of philosophical theories of the emotions, theories that precisely try to conceive of the emotions as partly or wholly constituted by cognitive states. We shall start by considering the connections between emotions and beliefs. This will lead us to examine an attempt to analyze the emotions in terms of beliefs and desires (the mixed theory). As we shall see, this approach faces a variety of important difficulties, which will lead us to consider a second and closely related account of the emotions. According to this account, emotions are not combinations of beliefs and desires, but rather representations of how our desires fare. We shall argue that this second theory faces no less serious difficulties. As a whole, this chapter tries to show that the fact that emotions motivate us in all sorts of ways does not support the idea that they should be understood in terms of desires.

## Emotions and beliefs

As we have already stressed, all emotions – whether basic or nonbasic – are triggered by certain events, objects, or situations and their features. More-over, these events, objects, or situations are not only the causes of emotional responses in the way solar rays cause sunburn; in principle, the subject who feels an emotion apprehends in one way or another the situation or the object which triggers this emotion. That is why, as we have seen, it can always be sensibly asked what we feel such and such an emotion *about*. In the jargon of contemporary philosophy, we say for this reason that emotions are intentional phenomena, i.e. they have the property of being directed at something. If the dog frightens Jonas, the latter must then in some way have a representation of the dog. This is to say, as we have already seen, that emotions have cognitive bases. Typically, this idea has been straightforwardly understood as implying, say, that if Jonas is afraid of the dog, he must have a certain belief or make a certain judgment about the dog. Hence it is essential to gain a grasp of the relations between emotions and beliefs.[1]

Consider the two following examples. Jonas believes that he is facing a dog that is baring its teeth and preparing to pounce. He is afraid. Mary believes that her cat has had a serious accident. She is sad. On the basis of such examples, it may seem that the awareness of certain facts is not only presupposed by certain emotions – something we already acknowledged in Chapter 1 – but necessary and sufficient for their occurrence. The thesis in question may take the form of the claim that an emotion is nothing but the presence of beliefs or judgments of this kind.

However, it is easy to see how such an identification of emotion and belief will be far from satisfactory. The principal point is that, if Jonas is, say, a dog trainer, and Mary longs to get rid of her old incontinent Persian, there is no reason to think that the beliefs mentioned above are any more to be identified with the emotions of fear and sadness than for instance amusement and relief. These considerations show that the suggested analysis is too naïve for a couple of reasons. First, as we have just remarked, it does not account for the specificity of emotions: the link between these sorts of beliefs and any particular type of emotion is too loose to individuate the latter. Second, an adequate analysis of emotions must be able to account for the fact that we constantly cite them when explaining behavior. Somehow emotions are more closely tied to *particular kinds* of motivations and behavior than the beliefs just alluded to. And that is why no short list of such beliefs can have the same explanatory role as emotions.

There are two common strategies that attempt to overcome these difficulties. The first introduces the notion of desire; the second invokes the notion of value. In this chapter, we shall consider the mixed theory as well as another theory that also emphasizes, albeit in a different way, the relation between emotions and desires. The discussion of the theories of emotions in terms of value cognition will occupy us from Chapter 5 onwards.

## The mixed theory

We pointed out in Chapter 1 that there are certain important differences between emotions and desires. Although in ordinary language we sometimes use the word 'desire' to refer to certain emotions (for instance, we might say 'Jonas desires to win the bingo draw' when what we mean is that he hopes to win it), identifying emotions with desires is not really an option. That is why there is no contemporary theory of the emotions that reduces them completely to desires. Nonetheless, several theories do accord desires a prominent place in the analysis of emotions.

The idea is to deal with the above-mentioned problems in the following way. If Jonas's and Mary's beliefs do not suffice to individuate their fear and sadness, it is because a specification of their motivational state is still lacking. In order for Jonas to be afraid, as a complement to his belief that he is facing a snarling crouching dog, we must add a desire to avoid being attacked by the dog. In order for Mary to be sad, we must add to her belief a desire to enjoy the company of her cat in the future and do whatever she can to keep it alive. This thesis, the central contention of the mixed theory, amounts to identifying emotions with combinations of beliefs and desires (e.g., Green 1992, Searle 1983).

Recall that one important intuitive difference between emotions and desires lies in the fact that the latter have the world-to-mind direction of fit: desiring is being in a state that inclines the subject to alter the world so as to make it fit her representation of the desired state of affairs. So a complete assimilation of emotions to conative phenomena should be resisted. However, the mixed theory avoids this problem insofar as the beliefs it appeals to have the opposite direction of fit, a direction that corresponds to the manner in which we assess emotions. This echoes what we said in Chapter 1, when we observed that we assess the emotions as correct and incorrect, as justified and unjustified, and the same is, of course, true of beliefs. And in this way the present theory kills two birds with one stone. On the one hand, it accounts for the specificity and variety of our emotions: the content of the beliefs and the desires is fine-grained enough to account for the distinctiveness of each and every emotion. On the other hand, the introduction of desires into the analysis allows us to explain the close link between emotion and behavior. Their respective desires account for why Jonas will for instance clamber up the nearest tree and Mary will take her cat to the vet.

This strategy can then be seen as an application to the particular case of emotions of the general schema, which holds that all action is the result of a combination of conative and cognitive states. For instance, Arthur's anger at Alison is nothing but his belief that she has insulted him coupled with his desire to take revenge. Naturally, to analyze all the various emotions, a mixed theory will have to invoke some relatively complex combinations of beliefs and desires. For instance, it has been suggested that hoping that P could be analyzed in terms of the absence of the belief that P, the absence of the belief that not-P, the belief that it is possible that P and the desire that P (Searle 1983: 32).

We should also highlight two further potential virtues of this theory. One consequence is that emotions are not a *sui generis* category of mental states, since on this account they are reducible to specific combinations of other kinds of mental states. Studying the emotions thus turns out to be nothing more than the study of the familiar categories of desire and belief. The theory also fits snugly into a general framework of psychological explanation, which has proven so successful in numerous domains of philosophy: belief–desire psychology.

Nonetheless, the few remarks in previous sections about the nature of desire suffice to raise doubts about the soundness of this theory. In particular, we emphasized that desires are always directed at states of affairs, and that they are constitutively linked with the subject's belief that she can do something to bring about what she desires, whereas emotions are not always directed at states of affairs and exhibit a much looser connection with action. So Jonas's contempt for Mike, an episode, seems to be about an object and not a state of affairs; and Mary's regret concerning the bad weather has at best very indirect links with anything she could do. These cursory remarks suggest at the very least that introducing desires in the analysis of emotions is not the hoped for solution. Does this mean that these two difficulties force us to dismiss the mixed theory despite its many advantages? Not necessarily.

The best way to deal with the first difficulty is simply not to let oneself be impressed by the claim that emotions may be intentional relations to objects that cannot be understood in terms of intentional relations to states of affairs. After all, it is far from clear that Jonas's contempt for Mike is not specifically directed at one or many states of affairs involving Mike. In this connection, one may also note that, since the surface grammar of 'desire' also makes it sometimes look as if desires were intentional relations with objects ('Mike desires a Ferrari'), perhaps there is likewise reason not to take the grammar too seriously in the case of emotion terms taking nominal complements.

As regards the second difficulty, the natural option is to broaden the class of conative phenomena that the theory can appeal to. For, if having the world-to-mind direction of fit is the mark of conative states, desires constitute arguably only one type of conative states, among which we also find wishes on the one hand and lower-level motivational states such as urges, drives, and aversions on the other. A sudden sexual urge is not easily assimilated to a propositional state. And wishes seem especially relevant for dealing with the second difficulty, since they, unlike desires, are often directed at past events and thus not directly related to the possibility of action.

When the class of relevant conative phenomena is expanded in this way, the mixed theory can furnish an account of those emotions that resisted analysis in terms of desires in the narrower sense. Along these lines, regret can now be understood as the belief that some event has occurred and the wish that it had not occurred. This strategy also improves the account regarding the case of Mary's sadness about her cat put forward earlier. One need no longer refer to her desire to enjoy the company of her cat in the future, a desire that in any case seems to be presupposed by the emotion and to motivate it rather than constituting part of it. One can more plausibly analyze Mary's sadness in terms of the wish that the accident had not occurred, a wish that may seem related to the emotion of sadness as a constituent element. Extending in this way the domain of motivational states to include wishes thus looks promising (Gordon 1987). Additionally, drawing attention to the existence of urges or appetites may have the further benefit of accounting for certain 'gut-level' emotional reactions in a way that appears intuitively more fitting. Certain cases of fear and disgust, for instance, will have as constituents some form of aversion for, respectively, bodily damage and putrefaction.

However compelling this form of the mixed theory may seem, we do not believe that it can meet the challenge of fully accounting for the variety of roles that emotions must play in a theory of mind. The mixed theory, we shall argue, misconstrues the explanatory relations between emotions and conative states.

We just emphasized the fact that the mixed theory can appeal to a broad array of conative states. For present purposes, it will be helpful to further distinguish amongst these states between desires with an 'open' content (e.g., in the case of fear: the desire to preserve one's physical integrity; in the case of anger: the desire to be respected; in the case of admiration: the desire to see artworks) and desires with a 'restricted' content (e.g., the desire to avoid being attacked by a particular dog or to run away from it; the desire not to be ignored by Jack or to hit him; the desire to see a particular Van Gogh painting or to continue seeing it). For now, let us work with an intuitive understanding of this contrast.

Drawing attention to this distinction makes it clear that many desires with a restricted content cannot be recruited by the mixed theory. To conceive of the desire to flee from the dog in the case of fear, or of the desire to hit Jack in the case of anger, as constituents of the relevant emotions, is simply misguided. These desires are obviously motivated by the respective emotions rather than parts of them: one desires to flee from the dog or to hit Jack *because* one is afraid of the dog or *because* one is angry at Jack.

But perhaps we have not selected the most suitable examples of desires with a restricted content. Fear of the dog might rather consist in the desire to avoid being attacked by the dog, anger at Jack in the desire not to be ignored by him, and admiration of a Van Gogh in the desire to see a Van Gogh. Whether or not one thinks that such desires are good candidates for being constituent parts of the emotions – and not, say, motivational states that explain why the relevant emotions occur – the following very general problem must be grappled with. Any satisfactory theory of the emotions must have the resources to explain what the different instances of an emotion type have in common. Now, while a mixed theory proceeding in terms of restricted desires may succeed, as we acknowledged, in individuating the different instances of an emotion type, it simply cannot account for what these instances have in common. There is clearly something shared by cases of fearing a dog, fearing that one has lost one's wallet and fearing that the speaker will not arrive in time, but nothing in the mental states that the mixed theory appeals to can account for why these three emotional episodes belong to the same emotion type. In a nutshell, if this version of the mixed theory were the best we could come up with, it would be grist for the mill of those who think that emotions do not form interesting psychological categories, an idea we have seen should be resisted (Chapter 2).

By contrast, appealing to desires with open contents will allow the mixed theory to provide an account of what the different instances of an emotion type have in common. Indeed, such desires can more straightforwardly be associated with each emotion type. For instance, there is a close tie between fear and the desire to avoid physical harm, between sadness and the desire not to lose something dear to us, between anger and the desire to be respected, and between admiration and the desire to see aesthetic objects. On this amended version of the mixed theory, emotions would then be combinations of desires with open contents and the relevant belief of the subject about her circumstances. This may not only allow us to individuate emotion types, it may also account for the manner in which emotions give rise to desires with a restricted content: Jonas's desire to avoid being attacked by the dog will now be explained by his fear, i.e. by his desire to avoid physical harm and his belief that there is an unpredictable dog in front of him.

Unfortunately, this way of solving the problem immediately gives rise to a new one. Notice how replacing desires possessing a restricted content with desires possessing an open content thereby removes the internal link we had between the contents of the beliefs (e.g., that the dog is going to attack me) and the restricted contents of the desires (e.g., to avoid being attacked by the dog) constituting the emotions. The version of the mixed theory in terms of beliefs (e.g., that the dog is going to attack me) and desires with open contents (e.g., to avoid physical harm) appeals to psychological states whose contents are disconnected from one another. For this reason, it is simply insufficient to account for the emotions. Indeed, until the subject grasps that the content of his belief is relevant to the content of his open desire, we are not in the presence of an emotion. Jonas may believe that a dog is capricious but this feature of the situation fails to inform his desire to avoid harm. In that case, he would simply not feel fear. An analysis of the emotions as combinations of desires with open contents and beliefs as a result falls short. And given that emotions are analyzed in terms of potentially disconnected beliefs and desires, this blocks any possibility of appealing to the emotions in order to explain the desires with restricted contents that we said are typically motivated by them.

The pressing question, then, is this: by means of which psychological states are the subject's beliefs about the particular situations she faces apt to motivate her to form desires with restricted contents in the light of her desires with open contents? The wished-for bridging psychological states must represent the relevance of these particular situations for her desires with open contents. While it seems to us that we cannot make progress on this issue within the framework of the mixed theory, this does not mean, as we shall now see, that we should give up the project of analyzing the emotions in conative terms. Still, we must conclude that the various forms of the mixed theory we have reviewed seriously misrepresent the explanatory relations between emotions and conative states. This conclusion is enough for our present purposes, but we shall revisit the mixed theory in Chapter 5, when we lay out different and very revealing objections that emerge from a focus on phenomenology.

## The desire satisfaction/frustration approach

The lesson of the preceding section is then not necessarily that desire has no significant role in an account of emotions. Rather the mistake may lie in conceiving of desires as constitutive parts of them. The discussion so far seems to suggest that desires should be detached from the emotions but nevertheless understood as being essential ingredients in an explanation of why emotions occur. This strategy would consist in an approach to the explanatory relations between open desires, emotions, and restricted desires in line with the conclusions we reached in the preceding section: open desires explain why we feel emotions, and emotions themselves mediate between open desires and the restricted desires we come to form in the circumstances. Adopting this strategy will allow us to say that Jonas's desire to avoid physical harm explains why he is now afraid, and that his fear in turn explains why he wants to flee. Within such a framework, the emotions themselves would be recruited to constitute the wished-for bridging psychological state that was missing within the mixed theory. Now, according to a small but important family of theories located squarely within a conative approach to the emotions, emotions are ideally suited to play this bridging role because they are in fact representations of the fates of our desires (e.g., Schroeder 2006, Wollheim 1999).

Recall the manner in which we distinguished desires from emotions. We saw that desires have a world-to-mind direction of fit, that is to say, that desires aim at changing the world so it comes to match the desired state of affairs. When this matching occurs, we speak of a desire being 'fulfilled' or 'satisfied'. When it does not, we say that the desire is 'frustrated'. Now, the satisfaction or frustration of our desires is not only something that happens, it is also something we are especially given to thinking about. I realize I did not get the prize I desired, I am aware that I am finally soaking in the bath I longed for.

Note first that, as opposed to desires themselves, representations of the fate of our desires have the mind-to-world direction of fit that we argued previously was characteristic of the emotions: their correctness hangs on whether the relevant desires are indeed satisfied or frustrated. It should be observed, second, that such representations of the fate of our desires presuppose – barring cases of misrepresentation – that we have the relevant desires and, for that reason, these representations can play a bridging role between antecedent motivations and subsequent ones. It is, say, because Jonas realizes that his desire to avoid physical harm is likely to be frustrated in the situation in which he finds himself that he forms the subsequent desire to flee at once. Note, finally, that this approach to the emotions furnishes an immediate explanation of what we referred to in Chapter 2 as the valence or polarity of the emotions: positive emotions are those that represent desires as being satisfied, negative emotions are those that represent them as frustrated.

The foregoing observations point towards an interesting approach: emotions should be analyzed as representations of desire satisfaction or frustration. The idea can be cashed out in more or less elaborate forms and has been espoused by philosophers approaching the emotions from very different theoretical perspectives. For example, Schroeder, an empirically minded philosopher, thinks of affect as being essentially, though perhaps not solely, the representation of 'change in desire satisfaction relative to expectations' (Schroeder 2006). The pleasure I get from having climbed this mountain's face is to be understood along the following lines: my achievement triggers the thought that, on balance, the satisfaction of my desires is higher than I expected. In more recognizably intentional terms, Wollheim, a psychoanalytically inclined philosopher, conceives of emotions as attitudes we have concerning an object or event we perceive as the source of the satisfaction or frustration of a desire. I am angry at Mike, say, when I perceive the way he drives as potentially or actually frustrating my desire to be on time at the concert (Wollheim 1999: Lecture 1). Both Schroeder and Wollheim emphasize the link between these representations of the fate of our desires and the pleasures or displeasures that accompany our affective lives. While Wollheim speaks of the relevant attitudes as being 'tinged' with pleasure or displeasure, Schroeder outright identifies pleasures and displeasures with the aforementioned representations.

There is much to be queried in the general approach to the emotions that these theories suggest. Our discussion and criticism here will be directed at the general framework in which they are embedded, and not at the specific versions to which we have just alluded. First, a striking feature of the desire satisfaction/frustration approach is that it apparently sees the emotions as metarepresentations, i.e. as intentional states having other intentional states as objects. Feeling an emotion would then require the capacity to represent desires and complex facts about them, which will strike many as not very plausible. Of course, it is possible to think of these metarepresentations as operating at the subpersonal level, but then we seem to give up on the task that many philosophers in the domain take themselves to be pursuing, that of shedding light on emotions understood as first-person experiences.

Second, granting that the approach is one whose target is to account for emotions as experiences, we may also question whether it is able to capture their phenomenological variety and richness. Appealing to a representation of desires as satisfied or frustrated in the analysis of emotions strongly suggests that we should approach their phenomenology in terms of what it feels like to have one's desires satisfied or frustrated. Whether or not we understand desire satisfaction and desire frustration as pleasure and displeasure, it is doubtful that this way of partitioning the phenomenological territory will allow us to capture the extreme variety of ways emotions make themselves experientially manifest. At the very least, something beyond the mere phenomenology of frustration will be required to distinguish, for instance, emotions such as fear, sadness, regret, and shame. All these emotions may well involve one and the same representation of a change in expected desire satisfaction, yet they clearly differ in their phenomenology. While none of these remarks as they stand constitute, in our opinion, sufficient grounds to reject the approach under discussion, some further considerations yield good reasons to cast doubt on its central tenets.

What the present approach shares with the mixed theory, at least in its most plausible version, is the claim that the existence of desires with an open content is essential to the explanation of all emotional episodes, although the role desires play in the resulting accounts of the emotions differs (the mixed theory regards them as constitutive parts of the emotions, the present approach as antecedent triggers). And claiming this much might not be warranted. Although it is plausible to point to the desire to preserve one's physical integrity as the biological basis around which fears congregate, the presence of the relevant desires for other emotion types is less obvious. In some cases of admiration, for instance the admiration we may feel in front of a painting the first time we are dragged to a museum, the claim that we must have an open desire to see works of art – the only desire of this nature we can appeal to in this connection – appears both implausible and insufficient. It is implausible, for even if we have such a desire, undergoing the resulting emotion entails on this account that our admiration represents this desire as being satisfied by the experience of the painting. Are we really to believe that the experience of being moved by a late Rembrandt is, as a matter of necessity, shot through with the realization that our deep-seated but vague desire is now fulfilled? This is doubtful. And even if most or all of our emotions were accompanied by representations of the fate of our desires, these representations do not seem to constitute the emotion itself but are more convincingly viewed as distinct mental states, namely as states that reflect on the potential sources of the emotion just experienced. That is, it seems that admiring a painting is one thing, realizing that our desire to look at works of art has been at last fulfilled another. And notice that when the open desire is salient – I am finally going to have time to indulge in my desire to see works of art – the awareness of my desire being now fulfilled competes with and sometimes even prevents the expected emotional experience from occurring.

It should be stressed that the present criticisms are premised on the fact that the version of the desire satisfaction/frustration approach under consideration, that offered for instance by Wollheim, has it that the emotion is partly constituted by the representation of the content of an open desire as frustrated or satisfied. That is what makes it implausible. One natural modification of the approach would then simply omit this constraint. For example, as Schroeder seems to view the matter, the emotion can be thought of as a representation whose content is that *overall* there is an increase or a decrease in one's desire satisfaction. On this version, while the subject is required to have the relevant open desire, the emotion does not have to contain the representation of this very desire. In fact, the subject does not even need to know that he has it.

Whether we think that this amendment contributes to making the desire satisfaction/frustration approach more plausible or not, the shortcomings of the overall framework come into view when it is approached from a different angle. The fundamental explanation of the emotions it offers is again insufficient. In the quest to explain the emotions, a desire is posited, but this desire in turn requires an explanation of exactly the same kind we were seeking about the emotions in the first place. Let us bring this chapter to a close by examining this important issue in some detail.

If we explain why a subject is moved upon seeing a given work of art by saying that he wanted to see works of art, this explanation may be causally relevant in explaining the onset of an emotion, but it is clearly uninformative as an elucidation of why he is moved in the specific way he is. For what must be explained is not simply the fact that he is moved, but, as the case may be, why he is positively moved – he feels admiration – when he lays his eyes on a late Rembrandt. And appealing to the subject's desire to see works of art will not suffice for these purposes, as is shown by the fact that some works of art will not move him positively at all. After all, it may well be the case that our subject will feel a positive emotion when facing a Rembrandt but not when facing a Bouguereau, something the theory should try to explain. At this point, in order to explain the subject's admiration, we may opt to appeal to a different desire with open content: the desire to see *beautiful* works of art. Yet this is tantamount to desiring to see admirable works of art.

It is important to note the occurrence of an evaluative term in the content of the desire postulated here. We started with the desire to see works of art and moved on to speak of a desire for beauty. It now seems as if what is required from the subject is that he is motivated to contemplate things insofar as they are beautiful. And it should be observed that, in our attempts at specifying which open desires are relevant for the different emotion types, we found ourselves already using evaluative terms: we traced anger back to an open desire to be *respected*, sadness to an open desire not to *lose what is dear to us*, etc. At this stage, we might well start to wonder whether open desires do not simply manage to play their allotted role in explaining emotions in virtue of being (disguised) *evaluations*. If this is what is ultimately going on in the approach under discussion, it appears to entail a complete reconfiguration of what desires are. In addition to – and in some cases perhaps even instead of – being states that aim at being fulfilled and so may turn out to be frustrated or satisfied (i.e. states with a world-to-mind direction of fit), desires now appear to represent some state of affairs or object as being worthy of pursuit or avoidance. That is to say that they are states of valuing or evaluations, i.e. states with a mind-to-world direction of fit.

This idea is not as fantastic as it might first appear, it can be traced back to a venerable conception of desires as representations of something 'under the guise of the good' (see Tenenbaum 2007, Schroeder 2009). What is important to note is the radical shift this conception of desires amounts to. For if the conative approach were compelled to fall back on such a conception of desire, then the initial promise that it could account for emotions exclusively in terms of the satisfaction or the frustration of an agent's aims has been broken. What we have been offered instead is an elucidation of emotions in terms of prior states of valuing, positively or negatively. Desires or aversions, insofar as they are appealed to in an explanation of the emotions, are now conceived of as representations of some object or state of affairs as good or bad. While such representations can be said to be correct or incorrect, it makes no sense at all, however, to think of them as being satisfied or frustrated (see Chapter 1). If this is the case, the central tenet of the present approach is found to be unsound.

Yet there may be a lesson to be drawn from this failure. The states of valuing, positively and negatively, which the theory ends up positing may indeed play an important role in explaining why the emotions occur, and this even if the emotions can no longer be understood as representations of these states as satisfied or frustrated. Perhaps emotions signal the presence of something good or bad in the light of what the subject values or disvalues. And we might want to call all these states of valuing that explain the occurrence of emotions 'desires', but note, then, that what governs this classification is simply the fact that they represent something positively or negatively. In particular, and given the points we made in this chapter, desires should here be conceived as potentially completely disconnected from any state of affairs the subject is inclined to bring about, i.e. from any course of action he may contemplate taking. And, upon reflection, it becomes clear that this cost was incurred as soon as we admitted wishes within the class of conative states in order to salvage the approach under discussion. If one favors, as we do, a more restricted and more informative account of what desires are – they are states that concern the subject's envisaged courses of action and that might end up being satisfied or frustrated – one then has reasons to draw some important distinctions amongst assorted states of valuing that explain why emotions occur. To anticipate a later discussion, we should include among these states those we already alluded to in Chapter 1, affective dispositions generally, and indeed desires conceived as inclinations to bring about changes in the world and that can turn out, for that reason, to be satisfied or frustrated. As we shall see, conceiving of desires as aiming in this way at fulfillment does not rule out the possibility of assessing them as correct or incorrect. In Chapters 7 and 9, we shall suggest that they are correct if what the subject aims at bringing about ought to obtain.

## Conclusion

In this chapter, we introduced and discussed two theories of the emotions that attempt to analyze them in terms of beliefs and desires. The various versions of the mixed theory, we argued, cannot individuate the different emotion types or constitute insufficient accounts of the emotions. This weakness led us to consider the idea that emotions are representations of the frustration or satisfaction of our desires. We argued that such an approach either proves unable to explain the emotions or leads to a conception of desires as states of valuing that is difficult to reconcile with its central tenet. This, together with the fact that important alternatives to the conative approaches we discussed in this chapter view emotions as specific types of evaluations, should spur us on to take a closer look at the relations between emotions and values. In the next chapter, we shall try to better understand the nature of values and their links with the emotions. This will put us in an ideal position to discuss the various conceptions of the emotions as evaluations from Chapter 5 onward.

## Questions and further readings

(1)   Why introduce wishes in the analysis of emotions?
(2)   What is the main difference between the two versions of the desire satisfaction/frustration approach?
(3)   Why think that what we have called desires with an open content are in fact states of valuing?

On the *mixed theory*, and in addition to Searle (1983: Chapter 1) and Gordon (1987), see Marks (1982) and, for a very elaborate version, Green (1992). For a recent account of emotions in terms of desires broadly conceived, see Maiese (2011).

For the full presentation of Schroeder's account of desires, see his 2004 work. Issue 45.1 of the journal *Dialogue* contains various discussions of his approach as well as replies by the author. The idea that emotions are metarepresentations of belief confirmation and desire satisfaction is developed within a computational framework by Reisenzein (2009).

The idea that desires are *representations of objects as valuable or disvaluable* has found three important contemporary advocates in Helm (2001), Oddie (2005), and Tenenbaum (2007).

## Note

1 In what follows, we shall indifferently use the terms 'belief' and 'judgment', the latter being commonly conceived as the overt or covert manifestation of the former.

# 4 Introducing values

As we advanced through the dialectical thickets of desire-based accounts in the last chapter, we presented and assessed an account of emotions that conceives of them as representations of the satisfaction or frustration of our desires. In discussing the reasons for being dissatisfied with this account, our attention was once again drawn to the intimate links between emotions and values. These links have as a matter of fact been stressed since antiquity, and almost all of the theories we shall examine in the remainder of this book conceive of the emotions as being or involving types of evaluations. In the present chapter, our aim is to motivate and clarify this fundamental idea. We shall first explain some of the substantial roles values may play in connection with the emotions and, second, examine whether the nature of values allows them to play these roles.

## Emotions and values

That there are intimate links between emotions and values seems to be obvious. Ordinary language corroborates the existence of such links insofar as to each emotion type there corresponds an evaluative predicate, one often derived from the name of the emotion in question, as when we say of something that it is 'shameful', 'disgusting', 'annoying', 'contemptible', 'admirable', 'amusing', or the like. According to the idea that emotions are types of evaluation, having an emotion amounts to apprehending the object of the emotion in evaluative terms. Feeling shame or amusement consists in apprehending a given object as, respectively, shameful and amusing. We shall see and assess in the chapters to come the more specific analyses of emotions as types of evaluations that have been put forward.

For present purposes, bear in mind that what philosophers mean by 'values' or 'evaluative properties' differs to some extent from the way 'value' is commonly used. First, philosophers speak of positive *and* negative values. Thus this term does not only denote things like beauty, courage, and solidarity, but also ugliness, cowardice, and selfishness. Second, values are not only conceived of as abstract political or personal ideals one is committed to upholding – liberty, fraternity, equality, loyalty, etc. – but as properties exemplified by concrete objects, situations, or events, and we shall shortly turn our attention to what this ultimately amounts to.

The main motivation for conceiving of emotions as apprehensions of evaluative properties resides in the following observation: beyond the multitude of particular objects towards which a certain kind of emotion can be directed, occurrences of an emotion type are unified by means of the evaluative properties that are conventionally called the *'formal object'* of that emotion type (Kenny 1963). For example, fear can be about a dog, an exam, the direction of the stock market (particular objects), but each individual occurrence of fear consists in the apprehension of the particular object as dangerous or threatening (formal object). Similarly, my nose, my social background, my stealing may be what my shame is directed at (particular objects), but in all these cases my emotion consists in apprehending these particular objects as shameful or degrading (formal object). More generally, the introduction of formal objects sheds light on the identity of the various emotions and allows thus for the individuation of the distinct types of emotions.

Introducing formal objects with regard to the emotions allows us to clarify a fundamental aspect of their intentionality, which has remained implicit up to now. As already emphasized, emotions are not only directed at particular objects, but they also seem to present them in a particular way. The appeal to evaluative properties as the formal objects of the emotions clarifies the sense in which emotions are ways of apprehending salient features of the environment. It also sheds light on a subject briefly broached at the beginning of our discussion, that is, the various ways in which emotions seem to be assessable as appropriate or inappropriate (see Chapter 1). Indeed, aside from the function of individuating emotion types just alluded to, invoking formal objects appears to be needed in order to specify the *correctness* conditions as well as the *justification* conditions of emotions. This allows us to say for example that Mary's anger is justified when she has good reasons to believe that the joke is offensive, but incorrect, say, because her anger happens not to fit the facts, since the joke is actually quite innocuous. Similarly, Jonas's fear may be assessed as justified if it is based on his apprehension of a certain danger, and, as it happens, as correct because he indeed faces a dangerous situation.

Note, however, the following crucial fact. If the idea that emotions evaluate in ways that are subject to standards of correctness and justification is to play any substantive role, the apprehension of a given value and the actual exemplification of this value must be to some extent independent from one another. The evaluative properties of the objects in the world cannot be, so to speak, merely in the eye of the beholder. When diagnosing Mary's anger as justified but incorrect, for example, we have presumed the truth of a quite substantial claim: that a joke can be offensive independently of the fact that Mary responds to it with anger. And this assumption would prove wrong-headed if, as some forms of subjectivism about evaluative properties have it, the offensiveness of a joke was existentially dependent on such a response. More generally, if talk of correctness and justification is to have any bite in relation to the connections between emotions and evaluative properties, then it must be possible for an emotion to occur in the absence of any exemplification of the corresponding evaluative property and, conversely, an evaluative property may be exemplified in the absence of the corresponding emotion. To establish the plausibility of such an objectivist framework, one in which, as we shall see, our emotions respond to mind-independent evaluative properties, we shall for the remainder of this chapter review and criticize some classical alternative positions which try to analyze evaluative properties in terms of emotional responses.

## Subjectivism about values

Many philosophers and laymen alike are wary of taking talk of evaluative properties too seriously. Despite the fact that we commonly and constantly describe the world in evaluative terms, there is a widespread opinion according to which evaluative properties are rather strange or mysterious sorts of things. Perhaps because they are not ordinary objects of perception and do not seem to be easily inferable from perception, or because the question whether they are exemplified in given circumstances often gives rise to long-standing and apparently insoluble disagreements, or because, as opposed to other ordinary properties, they stand in close connection with what we ought and ought not to do, many philosophers have tried to explain them away. And, given the intimate connections between emotions and evaluative properties, one obvious avenue to avoid any commitment to a world populated by them consists in regarding value talk as a mere reflection of the manner in which objects and situations emotionally impinge on us. For we may think there is here a neat and simple solution to a number of enduring puzzles at the heart of the philosophy of value.

On the crudest version of the idea that evaluative properties should be analyzed in terms of emotional responses, an object's dangerousness or offensive character consists in the fact that it elicits fear or anger. If Max admires a given painting, then the painting is admirable. And if Claudette does not admire it, then it is not admirable. Analyzing evaluative properties in terms of subjects' actual responses directly entails that the same object may be admirable for one subject but not for another, and for the same subject at one time but not at another. While this might be considered at first sight to be a problem, the suggestion seems to embrace the idea that we should relativize evaluative properties to specific subjects and times – the admirable character of the painting is analyzed in terms of the more complex property consisting in its being admirable for given subjects at given times. Here are two reasons to balk at this radical form of subjectivism.

First, while the view is in part motivated by the idea that it provides a good account of the fact that many disputes as to whether an object exemplifies a given evaluative property rage unabated, it now transpires that it cannot make sense of these disputes without also assuming that those engaged in them are completely confused. Participants to these disputes, when they go about checking their reactions against those of others, when they attempt to discount those subjective factors that might interfere in their judgments, when they appeal to general principles or put themselves in others' shoes, are simply acting on the deluded assumption that there is a substantive answer to the question as to whether or not a given evaluative property is exemplified. According to radical subjectivism, there is simply no room for the kind of disputes we believe we are often engaged in and to which we, erroneously as it transpires, attach so much importance (e.g., Blackburn 1998). Second, and in direct connection with the point just made, another implication of the present picture is that the very idea of improving one's epistemological standing vis-à-vis evaluative properties makes no sense. Claudette could not come to realize that the painting she does not presently admire is better than she first thought. If we subscribe to radical subjectivism, we should rather conclude that the painting has simply acquired a new property. The change in Claudette's emotional responses could not reflect the fact that she is now in a position to appreciate properties of the object that she previously failed to take into account. She simply cannot be wrong regarding whether or not the painting is admirable.

These problems may appear to be easily solved by a slight modification of the thesis without touching its basic tenets. Instead of analyzing evaluative properties in terms of actual emotional responses, one can appeal to *dispositions* of objects or situations to cause such responses (e.g., Smith 1989). The suggestion is that the painting is admirable if it has the disposition, in given circumstances, of eliciting admiration in given creatures, for instance in human beings.

This appeal to dispositions has the immediate virtue of opening a space between evaluative properties and emotional responses, allowing us thereby to make sense of possible mistakes in relation to evaluative properties and, consequently, of substantial disputes about their exemplification. The dispositionalist model can allow for the existence of situations in which one responds to an object in a given way when this object does not in fact possess the relevant evaluative property, as well as the existence of situations in which the object possesses the evaluative property in the absence of the relevant response. After all, an object that is disposed to cause a given sort of response may, for a variety of reasons, elicit a different response or no response at all. One may, for instance, fail to admire a work painted by a recalcitrant debtor although it is in fact beautiful (the relevant subjects are disposed to admire it), or conversely admire a picture by one's revered ancestor though it is in fact a daub (the relevant subjects are at best disposed to indifference). This therefore leaves ample room for disputes about whether a given response (or group of responses) is of the sort that the object is disposed to cause. The fact that the exemplification of evaluative properties is independent of any particular occurrence of an emotional response makes the subjectivism to which the dispositionalist model subscribes less radical than that implicated by the analysis of evaluative properties in terms of actual responses.

Although it looks as though we have resolved the problems attending the crudest form of subjectivism, the dispositionalist model remains, at this stage, very sketchy. A fully fledged version of dispositionalism must reach a decision as to which subjects should be appealed to, and, among their responses, which are to count as manifestations of the relevant dispositions. Does the admirable character of a work of art depend on its disposition to cause admiration in all and every creature, or only in those that show minimal interest in the fine arts, or perhaps only in established experts? And, of course, whatever class of subjects gets elected, the fact is that some of their responses (those elicited when the painting is badly lit, when the subject is moody, tired or in love with the painter, etc.) will fail to qualify as manifestations of the relevant disposition. Appealing to the classical and recurring figure of the impartial spectator (Smith 1790/1976) constitutes one attempt – notoriously hard to work up into something more than vague hand-waving – at specifying the relevant class of subjects and responses. Now, whether or not one succeeds in reaching a principled decision concerning the relevant subjects and responses, a central implication of dispositionalism should in our opinion lead us to reject any specific form it might take.

For, at the end of the day, the fact that a given object or situation possesses a certain evaluative property ultimately depends, according to dispositionalism, on a brute psychological fact – in this respect, the approach does not differ from the cruder form of subjectivism discussed above. Note in particular that a very problematic upshot of this approach is that the world could become a better place (with fewer evils) if future generations were simply inured to torture, poverty, slavery, etc., which are per hypothesis evils only due to our current indignant sensitivity to them. In other words, the space opened up by the dispositionalist approach between evaluative properties and emotional responses does not allow for a satisfactory account of what we mean by correct or incorrect emotions. In line with this diagnosis, the views that we are going to discuss all agree with the idea that the existence of a widespread and stable disposition to have a certain emotional response is compatible with the absence of the relevant evaluative property.

## Fitting attitude analyses

Retreat from these subjectivist positions for the reasons we have presented does not necessarily mean that one abandons the project of analyzing evaluative properties in terms of emotional responses. However, to do so, one cannot rest content with the emotional responses subjects are likely to have, but must add further constraints on those emotional responses conscripted into the analysis of evaluative properties. The observation that the actual distribution of dispositions to respond need not match the distribution of evaluative properties might then prompt one to pursue the idea that the relevant emotional responses must be normatively qualified (Brentano 1889/1969).

What does this mean? An emotion is normatively qualified if it is *required* or *appropriate* given the circumstances in which the subject finds herself, i.e. if there are good reasons to endorse it. Admiration towards the painting is appropriate neither because the painting has the stable disposition to elicit admiration, nor because it has the primitive property of being admirable, but rather because of the existence of a norm or a set of norms stating that admiration towards it is required or appropriate. On the dispositionalist model, dispositions were introduced in order to filter out the responses relevant for the analysis of evaluative properties. This task is now delegated to a normative property of the responses themselves, which they have in virtue of the existence of norms stating that they are required or appropriate or fitting in the circumstances. This is the distinctive claim of the fitting attitude analysis of value (FA-analysis).

According to this analysis, the order of explanation thus goes from the appropriateness of a response to the evaluative property: for an object to have an evaluative property is for the related response to be appropriate. Typically, it is claimed that the FA-analysis helps demystify evaluative properties – in this respect it is comparable to the subjectivist approaches discussed above – while also furnishing distinctive grounds to concern ourselves with them, since evaluative properties are explained in terms of norms (Rabinowicz and Rønnow-Rasmussen 2004). But what does it mean for a response to be appropriate if we are discouraged from explaining this property by appealing to the relevant evaluative property? The task consists in isolating a set of norms that serves to measure the appropriateness of emotions while eschewing any reference to the evaluative properties of their objects. This is by no means easy, but two plausible options come to mind.

The first option consists in looking for these norms in the biological functions the emotions supposedly have for the relevant creatures (e.g., Ruse and Wilson 1986). The norms relevant for measuring the appropriateness of emotions would, on this view, be teleological in nature, i.e. they would emerge from the biological function performed by these responses. An emotion is appropriate if it promotes the biological fitness of its subject (or alternatively that of the subject's social group or some of its genes). One will then say that fear of tarantulas is appropriate for humans, whereas fear of European spiders is not, since responding in the latter way does not correspond to the function assigned to fear by our biological make-up: avoiding physical harm. Similarly, shame might be said to be appropriate when it functions to appease other members of the group and helps heal or restore interpersonal relationships, and inappropriate when it leads to isolation and ostracism. The hope is that there exists for each emotion type a specific norm encapsulating the manner in which it is adaptive, a norm that serves to measure the appropriateness of specific emotional occurrences. This option contrasts with the dispositionalist approach in that a response that favors biological fitness is not necessarily statistically prevalent (it can be rare amongst the members of a species), and conversely a statistically prevalent response can run counter to such fitness.

Beyond the difficulties that arise as soon as one seeks to determine biological functions, note that the domain we are here concerned with renders this endeavor peculiarly complex. If the function of the heart is clear, those of the yearnings housed therein are much less so. These considerations aside, let us recall the point of introducing normative qualifications into the analysis in the first place. The aim was to account for the possible divergence of evaluative facts and responses, and we may doubt that the option under discussion can fulfill it. The fact that a response favors fitness – especially if fitness is measured at the level of the gene – is indeed often quite divorced from the evaluative considerations that we think bear on the circumstances and guide the way we actually measure the appropriateness of the response. Whether or not my present shame at what is in fact a laudable accomplishment contributes to appease the other members of my group, and facilitates my continued integration within it or the survival of my genes, as the evolutionary psychology trope would have it, shame at such accomplishments is generally inappropriate. Similarly, hostility towards foreigners might well have favored the fitness of some individuals, groups, or genes, yet this fact seems totally irrelevant to determining whether it is correct to respond to foreigners in this way.

The option we just reviewed appeals to teleological norms that are not of the kind we readily invoke to measure the appropriateness of emotions. The second option within the FA-analysis that we shall now consider consists in elucidating the appropriateness of emotions by means of other norms – rational norms – that we invoke or could invoke in their favor. There are emotions we reflectively endorse because we think that they are reasonable in the circumstances, and others we discard because we consider that there exist reasons not to respond in these ways. For instance, we readily assess indignation towards cold-blooded murder and admiration of Leonardo's *Virgin of the Rocks* as appropriate responses, and consider that fear of mice or anger at a perfectly innocent remark ill-behooves well-adjusted adults. The relevant reasons might be readily accessible or require a more complex process of determination relying on institutions, experts, and significant deliberation (Wallace 2010). However complex the process, the important point for present purposes is the idea that there exists a set of reasons with the requisite normative force, i.e. reasons that when available render the emotion reasonable or appropriate.

Since the account under discussion is a variant of the FA-analysis, remember that on this view reasons and the relevant type of normativity have explanatory priority over evaluative properties: the object has the relevant evaluative property in virtue of the existence of reasons that make the emotion appropriate. Accordingly, one should say that something is dangerous or admirable because there are reasons to respectively endorse fear or admiration towards it, and hold in check one's inclination to say that fear or admiration are appropriate because the object is dangerous or admirable. This is why the relevant reasons and norms should be specified in complete isolation from evaluative properties, on pain of rendering the whole project viciously circular. Yet, is it possible to specify them independently of any reference to evaluative properties?

The problem is not easily sidestepped, since it does not take too much thinking to realize that there are different sorts of reasons for which we endorse or reject emotions, and so a variety of ways in which an emotion can be perceived as appropriate (see Chapter 1, pp. 6–7). Recall the example in which we are asked to imagine that, in the course of a dinner, a joke is told at the expense of one of the guests (D'Arms and Jacobson 2000). If the joke is a good one, then surely amusement would be the appropriate response. Suppose, however, everyone agrees that, on balance, there are stronger reasons not to feel amusement in the circumstances – after all, the joke is cruel, likely to hurt one of the guests, and so amusement would be inappropriate. Or, to take a more dramatic illustration, suppose that we all had to feel admiration for a vile demon reigning over us on pain of facing some horrific torture. In such a case, we all would have excellent reasons to admire the demon and this response would to that extent be reasonable or appropriate (Rabinowicz and Rønnow-Rasmussen 2004).

These examples draw our attention to the variety of reasons and rational norms – moral norms in the case of the joke, prudential norms in the demon case – which may undergird our assessment of an emotion as reasonable or appropriate. However, not all these reasons and norms will play an equal role in an attempt at analyzing evaluative properties: there being solid reasons to take a dim view of amusement in the joke case does nothing to suggest that the joke is not funny – it may even be hilarious. Likewise in the demon example, the demon remains vile and not in the least admirable despite the presence of overwhelming reasons to endorse admiration. The lesson is that the suggested analysis is flawed. It does not specify *in which sense* a response must be reasonable or appropriate when fixing the object's evaluative property. All of the mentioned responses conform to certain rational norms, yet they do not help fix the relevant evaluative facts.

Is a specification of the relevant reasons and norms forthcoming within the framework of an FA-analysis? Since the issue is a matter of ongoing and very sophisticated debate, we shall not embark on a detailed discussion of the various options that have been explored in the recent literature. What we shall more modestly offer is a brief discussion of two attempts, whose failure appears to us symptomatic of the difficulty facing any proposed specification of the relevant reasons in a plausible and non-circular way.

The first proposal consists in marking off the relevant class of reasons by observing that the 'right kind of reasons' are those that tend to immediately produce the corresponding response in us. The idea, developed by Parfit (2006), is that the reasons that make anger, fear, or admiration appropriate in the sense needed by the FA-analysis are those reasons, which, when brought to our attention, tend to immediately produce these emotions. By contrast, the prudential or moral reasons one may have for these emotions will not do so. Suppose that some aspects of *The Virgin of the Rocks* tend to immediately produce admiration; this shows, according to the present idea, that these features should be counted amongst the reasons that make admiration appropriate. Conversely, the fact that the demon will punish us if we do not admire him does not tend to immediately produce admiration, but at best tends to motivate the adoption of an indirect strategy aiming to foster such a response; this is why these reasons fail to qualify as reasons that make admiration appropriate. While a solution along these lines is intuitive and seems attractive at first, it will not resolve the present difficulty facing the FA-analysis. Indeed, Parfit's solution appears rather to constitute a return to the dispositional approach: after all, it claims that something has a given evaluative property insofar as it is disposed to immediately produce the relevant emotional response. And the fact that the response is qualified as immediate does not help alleviate the problems we have already touched upon: according to the view under discussion, it is also true that the world would become a better place if we were simply rewired so that some revolting facts did not tend to immediately arouse our indignation.

The second attempt at locating the 'right kind of reasons' within the FA-analysis consists in distinguishing, on the one hand, reasons related to the *content* of a certain attitude regarding a certain object and, on the other hand, reasons tied to the *attitude* regarding the object. The idea is that, in the demon case, we have 'reasons in favor of having an attitude' (admiring the demon), but no 'reason in favor of the content' of the attitude (the demon is admirable). And, in the joke case, we have reasons against the attitude (amusement), but reasons in favor of its content (the joke is amusing). On the basis of these observations, one may then suggest that the reasons relevant for the analysis of evaluative properties are reasons in favor of the content of the attitudes, and not those for the attitudes themselves. That is to say, when there are reasons in favor of the content of the attitude, the latter is reasonable or appropriate in a distinctive sense, the sense needed to get the FA-analysis on the right track (Danielsson and Olson 2007). This appears to go in the right direction, but is it compatible with the FA-analysis of eva-luative properties? That is to say, are the above reasons in favor of the content of the attitude really specified in complete isolation from these properties?

On its face, the account now looks quite suspicious. It seems to be saying that an object is admirable if and only if it provides reasons in favor of the content of admiration, i.e. in favor of representing it as admirable. This boils down to the claim that the relevant reasons are those that make the content of admiration correct, i.e. that make it the case that the correctness conditions of this content are satisfied. Now, while this indeed allows one to determine the subset of reasonable or appropriate responses relevant to the fixing of the object's evaluative property, this really seems to get us nowhere.[1] Indeed, without further specification of the nature of these correctness conditions, we are left with the hardly informative claim that the reasons relevant for the FA-analysis of evaluative properties are those reasons that make the content of the relevant response correct. This looks more like a way of restating the problem than a way of resolving it. And if we try to be more informative, then it seems difficult to avoid going against the whole spirit of the FA-analysis. Far from being normative in any substantial sense, the notion of correctness at issue here appears to be the same as the semantic notion we readily appeal to in relation to other mental states, whereby a response is correct if it repre-sents a given object as it is (Mulligan 2007, Salmela 2006, Tappolet 2011).[2] In other words, *contra* the FA-analysis, the specification of the relevant reasons does not appeal to normative properties of the response, but rather to those evaluative properties of the object that it was supposed to analyze.[3] After all, it is because objects are admirable that admiration towards them is a correct response. If so, then it is ultimately the evaluative properties of the object rather than a property of the emotional response that are appealed to in order to fix the relevant class of responses: appropriate or reasonable emotions are evaluations that justifiedly represent their objects as having the relevant evaluative properties.

## Forms of value realism

In the preceding, we have examined a selection of the many attempts to analyze evaluative properties in terms of emotional responses. Since all these attempts appear to suffer from serious flaws, we are led to the conclusion that, even though there are very intimate links between emotions and evaluative properties, this should not encourage us to try to analyze the latter in terms of the former. Before we wrap up this discussion, we shall say a few words about the family of approaches to evaluative properties we think the above observations support and the worries they face.

These approaches are predicated on the claim that evaluative properties are independent of emotional responses. And this suggests that the nature of these properties should rather be understood as being tied to the natural properties of the objects that exemplify them. Now, it is widely held that this relation is constrained by what is sometimes called the universalizability of evaluative properties vis-à-vis natural properties: if an object with certain physical properties exemplifies a given evaluative property, then a perfect duplicate of this object will also exemplify it (Moore 1903). To illustrate: suppose that a certain distribution of wealth is fair. A distribution exemplifying the same natural properties (an identical allocation across the population, etc.) will then also be fair. In this sense, a given distribution of natural properties determines a given distribution of evaluative properties. We say in such a case that the evaluative properties *supervene* on the natural properties.

This latter claim does not, as such, give rise to any definite theory of what evaluative properties are, but rather a sort of abstract schema that has to be filled in so as to lead to a more substantive theory. For there are not only various forms of supervenience, there is also no consensus as to the consequences of these various forms of supervenience for reducibility. Does the fact that evaluative properties supervene in this or that way on natural properties mean that the former are identical to the latter? Note in this connection that if evaluative properties are identical to natural properties, then the identity holds with respect to quite peculiar natural conditions. At the natural level, Hume's prose, the stride of a gazelle, and the Piazza Navona do not seem to share interesting properties, even though they are all properly described as elegant. The natural condition on which elegance supervenes is then likely to be a highly disjunctive one, which can be captured by saying that to be elegant is to exemplify either some of the natural properties of the leaping gazelle *or* some of Hume's prose, etc.

Can we say that such a highly disjunctive set of natural conditions is a natural property? If you take a liberal view of properties, you ought to answer in the affirmative and, as a result, you may conclude that evaluative properties are identical to these gerrymandered natural properties. If, however, one opts for a stricter conception of what can count as a property (rejecting in particular the idea of highly disjunctive properties), then the likely conclusion is that, while supervening on natural properties, evaluative properties are not identical to them: they are *sui generis* properties distinct from the natural properties on which they supervene.

## Conclusion

For present purposes, we do not need to adjudicate between these two forms of realism about evaluative properties. The aim was the more modest one of illustrating the sort of realism about evaluative properties that the problems related to analyses of them in terms of emotional responses might lead one to embrace. Subjectivism about values, whether in its radical or in its more moderate dispositionalist guise, did not strike us as a compelling way of removing the alleged mystery surrounding the existence of values. And we have given reasons to think that, in this respect, FA-analyses do not fare any better.

If we are on the right track with this train of argument, evaluative properties exist independently of emotional responses. As a consequence, reference to such properties in connection to the correctness and justification of emotions has the same import as it has in connection with other mental states and mind-independent properties. As we shall see later in this book, this conclusion will allow us to elaborate an appealing account of the conditions under which emotions may be thought to be justified (see Chapter 8). Let us also mention here that the fact that evaluative properties cannot be reduced to talk in terms of emotions in no way undermines the idea that emotions have a privileged epistemological role to play as regards our apprehension of values; quite the opposite in fact, as we shall see in Chapter 10.

## Questions and further readings

(1)   What is the formal object of an emotion and what roles does it play in emotion theory?
(2)   What are the different forms of subjectivism about evaluative properties and which problems do they face?
(3)   What difficulties does the existence of various sorts of reasons for the emotions create for the fitting attitude analysis?

On the introduction of the notion of *formal objects* in the contemporary literature on the emotions, see Kenny (1963). For serious misgivings regarding the usefulness of the notion, see Deigh (1994). In psychology, the equivalent notion is discussed under the label 'core relational themes'. See for example Lazarus (1991: in particular Chapter 3). Teroni (2007) offers a detailed account of the role of formal objects in the theory of emotions.

The source of *dispositionalism* about evaluative properties is sometimes thought to be David Hume (1975: 285–94). For contemporary accounts along dispositionalist lines, see Lewis (1989) and Smith (1989, 1994). For a dispositionalist or response-dependent approach to moral values, which is especially clear about its anti-realist consequences, see Prinz (2007). An important criticism of dispositionalism as well as an endorsement of realism about evaluative properties is provided by Johnston (2001).

Franz Brentano (1889/1969) is often held to be the father of the *fitting attitude analysis* of values, and Ewing (1947, 1959) is a vocal advocate of the view. McDowell (1985) and Scanlon (1998) constitute the most influential recent endorsements of this approach. For a detailed history of the FA-analysis of value and the different forms the theory can take, see in particular Rabinowicz and Rønnow-Rasmussen (2004). Louise (2009) and Reisner (2009) offer very helpful critical discussions of the various options within this framework.

While the thought that the appropriate character of an emotion is to be understood in terms of its biological function might be thought to originate with Aristotle, the specific framework in which this thought is pursued in the contemporary literature can be found in Frank (1988) and Cosmides and Tooby (2000).

For a family of views that tries to steer a middle path between dispositionalism and the FA-analysis, see the defenses of the so-called *no priority view* regarding the relation between evaluative properties and emotional responses in Döring (in press), Helm (2001), and Wiggins (1987).

On the different ways of interpreting the supervenience relation in the context of evaluative properties, see Jackson (1998), in particular Chapter 1. In the same book, Jackson defends the claim that evaluative properties reduce to natural properties. The alternative view according to which the existence of highly disjunctive bases of natural properties prevents reducibility is defended in Moore (1903) and, more recently and in greater detail, in Oddie (2005: Chapter 6).

## Notes

1 But see the further readings section of this chapter regarding the no-priority view concerning the nature of evaluative properties.

2 One may find further incentive to interpret 'appropriate' in this semantic sense, rather than in normative terms, in the fact that evaluative properties can be exemplified in varying degrees (things can be more or less beautiful, dangerous, or offensive). By contrast, something either is or is not 'required' (a feature true of all norms).

3 Note in this connection that there may be a norm enjoining us to have correct attitudes, and in this sense the satisfaction of correctness conditions is not normatively 'silent'. But this norm of course presupposes the semantic notion of correctness and so cannot serve to analyze it (Louise 2009: 352).

# 5    Emotions as value judgments

The discussions in the previous chapter have given us a better understanding of the nature of evaluative properties and their connections with the emotions. It is now time to consider how these connections can be put to use in order to analyze emotions. In prelude, let us step back for a moment to survey the dialectical situation we find ourselves in. In Chapter 3, we saw that conceiving of desires as constitutive parts of the emotions is the source of the problems facing the mixed theory. And relocating them as antecedents of the emotions in the way the desire satisfaction/frustration approach does did not improve matters. Now, remember that the difficulty that motivated us to consider desires in the first place was the fact that it proved impossible to individuate emotions by means of factual beliefs. Our discussion of conative theories of emotions knocked the pins out from under the notion that this difficulty could be removed by appealing to desires.

This diagnosis is shared by the rival theory of emotions we shall consider in this chapter. This classical theory, popular in antiquity (for instance, amongst the Stoics) and more recently brought back into fashion (e.g., Nussbaum 2004, Solomon 1993), holds that one can resolve this difficulty while retaining the idea that emotions are fully reducible to doxastic phenomena. It is only that the relevant doxastic phenomena are of a nature quite distinct from those involved in the theories we have considered up to now: they are *evaluative* or *axiological* beliefs. That is why it is called the evaluative judgment theory.

In this chapter, we shall first present and discuss this theory of the emotions. The fact that it faces a substantial difficulty will then lead us to discuss a common strategy to overcome it, a strategy that constitutes the so-called add-on theory of the emotions. We shall argue that this theory is no more convincing than the evaluative judgment theory, because it fails to do justice to the nature and role of phenomenology in emotions. Since this criticism relies on a substantial claim about the richness of emotional phenomenology, this will occasion a consideration of constructionism, an approach to the emotions rooted in a radical denial of this claim that amounts to a mirror-image version of the add-on theory.

## The evaluative judgment theory

To understand the distinctive claim of the evaluative judgment theory, let us return to the examples used at the beginning of Chapter 3. According to a proponent of the evaluative judgment theory, Jonas's belief that the dog has sharp teeth and Mary's belief that her cat has been injured are not sufficient to account for their respective fear and sadness. One needs to combine these beliefs not with further desires (as the mixed theory would have it) but with another kind of belief: Jonas's belief that the dog is *dangerous*, and Mary's belief that the death of her cat would constitute a significant *loss*. The crucial point here is that the beliefs now invoked are not neutral apprehensions of the world, but rather apprehend it in evaluative terms. Since only such beliefs render the respective attributions of fear and sadness intelligible, adherents of the evaluative judgment theory identify each emotion type with beliefs involving a corresponding evaluative property.

An immediate virtue of this theory is that it enables us to organize the class of emotions in a pleasingly straightforward manner – note that this virtue, like the others we shall consider, is shared by all theories that understand emotions as evaluations. The idea is that we can individuate each emotion type by means of a particular evaluative property (e.g., Roberts 2003: Chapter 3). And as we pointed out in the previous chapter, ordinary language corroborates the existence of such a link to the extent that each emotion type corresponds to an evaluative predicate, often one derived from the name of the emotion in question, as when we say of something that it is 'shameful', 'humiliating', 'annoying', 'contemptible', 'admirable', or the like. Feeling shame or humiliation amounts to believing that the object of the emotion exemplifies the related evaluative property. The theory thus holds the promise of allowing us to individuate the various emotion types. We have also seen that evaluative properties, conceived of as the formal objects of the emotions, play very important roles with regard to their intentionality. Remember that evaluative properties prove especially helpful in specifying the correctness conditions as well as the justification conditions of emotions. For instance, a reference to evaluative properties allows us to say that, on the one hand, Mary's sadness is *justified* if she has good reason to believe her beloved pet has died, and still maintain that, on the other hand, her sadness is incorrect because, unbeknownst to Mary, Snuggles in reality survived unharmed. Since the evaluative judgment theory holds that emotions are evaluative judgments, it is ideally suited to respect and account for all these important links between emotions and evaluative properties.

Beyond the virtues already mentioned, the evaluative judgment theory builds convincingly on the intuitively compelling idea that emotions have the mind-to-world direction of fit, i.e. aim at representing the world the way it is. In fact, it is only within the framework of this hypothesis that we can understand the central thesis of this theory according to which the different emotion types are different modes of evaluation.

A last selling point of the evaluative judgment theory is, in our view, the way in which it accounts for the links between emotions and motivation. This asset is not immediately clear, insofar as this theory completely assimilates emotions to doxastic phenomena. While the mixed theory, which reduces emotions to combinations of desires and beliefs, made these links too close to be satisfactory (see Chapter 3), it may seem that the evaluative judgment theory has the opposite problem of making the links disappear entirely. Yet there are at least two viable options.

The first consists in combining the theory with some form of *motivational internalism*, a view which holds that evaluative judgment – as distinct from factual judgment – is essentially motivating. To judge that the dog is dangerous is to be motivated to flee. To judge that one's nudity is degrading is to be motivated to disappear six feet underground. This solution nevertheless faces two difficulties. First, motivational internalism is not straightforwardly true: it seems possible for someone to sincerely judge that a given situation exemplifies some evaluative property without thereby being motivated to act (in the relevant way) – a point externalists about motivation like to insist on (see e.g., Smith 1994 and Alvarez 2010). Second, adopting internalism lays the evaluative judgment theorist open to the most immediate of the objections made in regard to the mixed theory. It renders the theory unable to account for those emotions that do not seem intimately related to action, for instance emotions directed at the past.

A second option amounts to fully taking on board the considerations that led us to reject conative approaches to the emotions. One of the main lessons was that an adequate theory must do justice to the idea that there exist important explanatory links between desires and emotions, and that, for this reason, we should not conflate the two sorts of states. The evaluative judgment theory can satisfy this demand in quite an elegant manner. You may remember that our query in the previous discussion was: what could for example explain a subject's desire to see beautiful works of art? The thought behind this question was that a desire with such an open content is in itself in need of an explanation. The present theory has a ready answer: the subject possesses such a desire because she judges that these works of art are admirable, or in other words, because she admires them. That is to say, emotions can now be regarded as reasons for certain desires without having a strict constitutive relation to them. Those emotions that are not intimately linked to action will for their part not engender any desire.

Let us now turn to the difficulties that arise for the evaluative judgment theory. The basic problem is quite simple. As has been often repeated in the literature on the subject, an evaluative belief is neither necessary nor sufficient for an emotion.

Consider first the objection regarding necessity. The claim that emotions necessarily imply evaluative beliefs is not compelling, for at least two reasons. A first worry is that it seems eminently possible or even commonplace to experience an emotion without making the kind of judgment required by the theory. Jonas believes firmly that this spider is not dangerous, yet he is terribly frightened. Mary is convinced that she has done nothing wrong, yet she is assailed with crushing guilt. Should we then, to save the theory, say that they in fact have contradictory beliefs, one of which is unacknowledged or unconscious, and in so doing, attribute to them a radical form of irrationality (Tappolet 2000, Peacocke 2004: 253–58, Döring 2009)? Conceiving of emotions as involving the attitude of belief, i.e. holding a proposition true, is clearly problematic. It simply does not seem correct to regard those situations, in which one believes that a given evaluative property is not exemplified yet undergoes the relevant emotion, as similar to situations in which one holds contradictory beliefs.

This difficulty may be circumvented, if, instead of doxastic states proper, we think of the emotions in terms of a less committed type of attitude towards the relevant proposition. One does not have to believe that the dog is dangerous in order to be afraid of it, but only to entertain the thought of its dangerousness (e.g., Greenspan 1988), or perhaps, as Robert Roberts would have it, to *construe* the dog as dangerous (2003: 69–83). As a result, Jonas could be afraid of the spider, i.e. construe the spider as dangerous, without being committed to the truth of the proposition that it is dangerous and so without exhibiting any form of irrationality, or at least none that is too severe.

While this certainly seems to go in the right direction, and regardless of how this notion of 'construal' is fleshed out, the real trouble regarding necessity might not be as yet fully put to rest. For, second, attributing beliefs or construals, and *a fortiori* attributing evaluative beliefs or construals, might still be thought of as too demanding with regard to the cognitive capacities the subject is required to deploy. She must at least master the concepts that figure in the propositions she holds to be true or through which she construes the relevant situation. For example, we can only attribute to Jonas the belief that Mary's scarf is of Bolivian Alpaca wool, if he has some kind of idea what scarves, alpacas, and Bolivia are (i.e. if he is to some extent able to correctly identify them and think about them). Likewise, if he construes Mary as being offensive – the kind of construal identified with anger on Roberts's evaluative construal theory – then he must master the concept of offense. But must one necessarily master the concepts that the relevant evaluative thoughts involve in order to have an emotion? We commonly attribute emotions to animals and infants, though this clearly conflicts with such a requirement. Given a choice between dropping the idea that infants and animals have emotions, and dropping the evaluative judgment or construal theory, many would incline towards the latter.

If these problems are not serious enough, the further objection concerning the sufficiency condition is perhaps decisive. The charge is simple: one can have the kind of evaluative belief that the theory invokes without having the corresponding emotion. For example, if you believe that you have done something degrading, it does not follow that you feel shame, nor does it follow that you feel indignation if you believe that such and such behavior is immoral. In everyday parlance, we might say that in some cases such beliefs, even if firmly held, leave us cold. I may believe quite firmly that it is dangerous to take a walk at this hour in this neighborhood, and yet feel no fear. An emotion is something that is felt, a feature we previously emphasized as we discussed the phenomenological nature of emotions. It is precisely this fundamental feature that the evaluative judgment theory seems to ignore. Note in passing that the same sort of objection can equally be directed at the mixed theory we considered in Chapter 3. Although I may believe that this expedition in the Sahara could seriously affect my health and want to keep my health, this is quite compatible with an absence of any phenomenology typical of fear. So claiming that emotions are nothing but combinations of beliefs and desires also fails to account for this feature.

## The add-on strategy

Let us assume it is possible to handle the objections regarding the failure of these theories to provide plausible necessary conditions for emotions, for example by watering down the notion of conceptual mastery (thus allowing for some such mastery amongst animals and infants). Which strategy should adherents of theories modeled on the propositional attitudes appeal to in order to deal with the objections concerning sufficiency? A natural and common strategy consists in patching things up by introducing a new component to their respective analyses of emotions. Thus modified, the evaluative judgment theory holds that only those evaluative judgments accompanied by a certain phenomenology constitute emotions. Such a strategy engenders theories that today are usually referred to – in a somewhat derogatory manner – as *add-on theories* (Goldie 2000: 40).[1] For instance, it is along such lines that Aristotle (1994: Book 2, 1–11), at least on some interpretations, defended a theory according to which emotions were evaluative judgments accompanied by pleasure or pain. The mixed theory, for its part, ends up being modified in a similar manner: only those combinations of beliefs and desires that are felt constitute emotions. Is this strategy a good way of accounting for the phenomenology of the emotions?

Let us first inspect the add-on strategy as applied to the mixed theory. This theory may on its face seem able to account for the phenomenology of emotions. It exploits the fact that desires combined with beliefs often have their own phenomenology; they are felt (Marks 1982). The most plausible candidates for felt desires are urges and appetites. Yet, it is not clear that such desires can be invoked for all emotion types (think, for instance, of nostalgia or hope), and they cannot at any rate, as we argued in Chapter 3, individuate the different types of emotions. This, you will recall, led us to claim that the only desires that are remotely plausible as constitutive components of the emotions apt to individuate them are desires with an open content (e.g., in the case of fear: the desire to preserve one's physical integrity, as opposed to the desire to avoid being attacked by a dog). If we were right to think so, then the present proposal seems entirely absurd. Such open desires are paradigmatic cases of dispositional (and thus inherently non-felt) desires (see e.g., Goldie 2000: 78–80). Thus the mixed theory cannot be salvaged in this way.

How about the modified version of the evaluative judgment theory? Insofar as it introduces the phenomenological dimension to complete the analysis, it raises questions about the respective roles it assigns to the phenomenological and the doxastic components of the emotions. On the one hand, the phenomenology might be regarded as impoverished, consisting for instance in nothing but a variation along a single dimension from pleasant to unpleasant, and as such it would not suffice on its own to individuate emotion types (Goldstein 2003, Whiting 2011). On the other hand, the phenomenology might be held to be sufficiently rich to distinguish emotion types. The two solutions each offer advantages and disadvantages, but neither is satisfactory.

The first solution has the virtue of attributing quite distinct roles to the two necessary conditions for emotions: the judgment individuates the emotion type, whereas the hedonic aspect accounts for its felt quality. Yet it does not allow us to do justice to the fine-grained phenomenological nuances of emotions. For instance, it would be a trifle bizarre to say that Jonas's grief at the death of his mother, and Jonas's anger towards his father, who is responsible for her death, both have the same phenomenology, and that only the different evaluative judgments distinguish them. The only possible defense, on such a theory of emotions, would be to appeal to the fact that evaluative judgments themselves possess a certain phenomenology. Although they do not have a phenomenology of a hedonic nature – recall that the theory precisely brings in pleasures and pains to account for this hedonic aspect – the judgments, all the same, may contribute in this way to the total phenomenology of emotions and so serve to individuate them.

The strategy is ingenious, and may at first seem plausible. However, it commits one to the existence of a phenomenology of judgment, and what is more, a phenomenology that varies according to the content judged – a proposal (see e.g., Strawson 2010: 339–44) that is far from evident. The difficulty can be illustrated in the following manner. Try to imagine an episode of your past affective life, for example an occurrence of shame. Make the corresponding evaluative judgment that, say, the situation was particularly degrading. While doing so, avoid feeling the negative hedonic quality characteristic of shame. This proposed exercise is perplexing: if one manages to not feel the unpleasant dimension of this emotion – and this is no easy feat – a cold judgment remains, one that appears to be in no way distinct from other evaluative judgments that correspond to emotions with different hedonic qualities. This thought experiment would seem to show the impossibility of hiving off the hedonic component of an emotion from its intentional phenomenology, however one goes about attempting to account for these features (but see Kriegel 2012).

The second solution has the virtue of accounting for these phenomenological nuances. It is hobbled, however, by a peculiar cumbrous complexity: it ends up assigning both the judicative and phenomenological components very similar, and hence potentially redundant, roles. An analogy may be helpful. If someone were to claim that perceptions are nothing but judgments (seeing a blue cube would accordingly consist in making the judgment that there is a blue cube in front of one), one would quite rightly complain that he has not accounted for the phenomenological dimension of visual perception (one may after all judge that there is a blue cube on the basis of a testimony). If he then introduces an experiential content that is sufficiently rich to account for the way objects and properties strike us when we see them (and not merely a collection of brute sensations that the judgment comes to inform), one will wonder if it would not be better to just jettison his initial suggestion, seeing as how the newly added elements could suffice on their own to account for perception.

Returning to the analogous case of the emotions, the judicative component seems similarly superfluous (recall how we established that the judgments introduced by the evaluative judgment theory may not be necessary for emotions). That is to say, the add-on approach taken to its logical conclusion ends up rendering the original proposal, which appeared to merely require some patching up, almost comically redundant; for it turned out that such a high degree of complexity was required of the added-on elements that they ultimately also seem capable of performing those functions that had initially made the positing of the primary and original components of the theory so appealing. Indeed, if the phenomenology is by itself able both to account for the qualitative component of emotions and to individuate the emotion types, why not simply consider this last suggestion as a basis for a theory that would reject entirely the cognitive program discussed here? To consider this in more detail, we shall turn in the next chapter to those theories that place the phenomenology at the heart of their analyses of emotions.

## Emotions as constructions

Before doing so, we must ascertain that we haven't disposed of what we have called add-on theories too quickly. While these types of theories are relatively rare in philosophy, they represent one major current in theorizing about emotions in psychology. In this family of views, which may be termed con-structionist theories of the emotions, an emotion is constituted by a feeling with a judgment tacked on: in this sense, the strategy at the heart of the add-on theory is turned on its head. The main motivation for such an approach rests on the denial of the intuition we used in the previous section to reject add-on theories that make use of an impoverished phenomenology. Recall that we argued that the intuitively rich phenomenological differences between emotion types weigh against the claim that an emotion could amount to a mere mixture of judgment and a generic positive or negative feeling. The family of theories that we are now considering is rooted in a radical alternative, the idea that the phenomenological dimension of emotion is too impoverished to serve as the basis for the fine-grained distinctions we think we can draw between different types of emotions. The following sort of example lends credence to this idea.

Suppose you tell me that two good friends of mine, Mary and Mike, were seen together at the party yesterday evening. At this news, I experience a mild internal flutter. To which I respond that it is good that they finally met. I think to myself, 'I am really happy that they met'. After a while, though, I come to suspect that my happiness was not as wholehearted as I first took it to be. At the end of the day, knowing as I do my friend Mike, I come to the conclusion that what I had felt was a bout of jealousy. There are many ways to model what is going on in such situations. According to the present approach, however, they suggest that emotions depend existentially on the subject's interpretation of the feelings she is experiencing.

This way of thinking about the emotions found its initial impetus in Schachter's and Singer's (1962) famous experiment in which subjects' physiological condition (altered through adrenaline injections) and what they apprehend as the cause of the feelings this condition elicits were independently manipulated. According to an influential interpretation (Mandler 1975), their results motivate the claim that the subject transforms her unspecified state of arousal into an emotion by categorizing her inchoate feelings in light of what she apprehends as having caused them, or more generally in the light of information available in the circumstances. This idea takes its most radical form in Barrett's 'conceptual act theory' of emotions, according to which an emotion occurs only when 'conceptual knowledge about emotion is brought to bear to categorize a momentary state of core affect' (Barrett 2006: 56).

Within this picture, the intentional object of the emotion, rather than being conceived as the cause and/or the object of the core affect or felt part of the emotion, is instead imposed by the subject on an otherwise objectless experience. Indeed, emotions have no object until the subject has investigated and decided what, if anything, the experience could be about. Note the crucial fact that on this view emotions are not *discovered* through conceptual inquiry and affective categorization to have a cause and an object. Rather, conceptual inquiry and categorization *constitute* or define what emotions are. What individuates an emotion is the decision the subject makes with regard to what she is going through and not some alleged intuitive and pre-theoretical ideas regarding their distinctive phenomenology. Protesting that the theory does not adhere to these pre-theoretical notions might then be perceived as missing the point entirely.

So, where does this leave us? A consequence of the view is a radical skepticism about the possibility of gaining anything but trivial knowledge about the emotions we feel. Indeed, it is difficult to see how the subject could be mistaken about the emotions she undergoes, for the theory provides no conceptual space here for a gap between what is really going on in someone's emotional life and the story that person chooses to tell herself about it. This conclusion should perhaps be resisted if alternatives exist that may explain the types of cases that motivate the view in the first place. This, we think, is possible through the use of three distinctions that we have already introduced.

First, many cases in which we think we are uncertain about what we feel are cases in which the uncertainty does not concern the present emotional episode, but rather the *affective dispositions* of which the present *emotion* is a manifestation. Is the joy I feel at Mary's breaking off her affair with Mike the expression of my being envious of their happiness or of my being in love with her? Doubts of this sort are indeed rather common. They do not warrant any constructionist conclusion, however. For they do nothing to show that the subject constructs her emotions by categorizing them, or to show that it is up to her to choose which affective dispositions they manifest. On the contrary, this is an aspect of affective life for which we quite rightly leave ample room for exploration, hesitation, mistakes, and discovery. Leaving no room for a gap between what is the case and the subject's conviction on these matters would leave us in a world without the possibility of self-deception.

Second, while the type of cases under scrutiny are indeed common and intriguing – we often reflect on what we feel and come to categorize it one way or another – it may not constitute the norm. What about the numerous situations in which our attention is not drawn to what we are feeling? Do we then not feel any specific emotions? In our opinion, constructionists blur the distinction between conscious and unconscious emotions discussed in Chapter 2. We are indeed often unconscious of our emotions in the sense that we would not, for a variety of reasons, be capable of categorizing them. That does nothing to support constructionism, however. For starters, we should question whether basing a theory of the emotions on this narrow subset of cases is warranted. In addition and more importantly, while this sense of the distinction between conscious and unconscious emotions does nothing to show that constructionism is wrong, it does offer us an alternative account of the sort of doubts or ignorance about our emotions that motivate this theory in the first place. And it does so in a way that is compatible with the claim that we undergo more than mere inchoate feelings when we are not indulging in affect categorization. To conclude on this issue, note that, in its rejection of the distinction between emotion and consciousness of emotion, the theory ends up requiring that a creature capable of emotions master complex metarepresentational capacities in order to feel specific emotions. One further consequence is then that animals and infants cannot have emotions at all, as they are unlikely to have the relevant conceptual knowledge about emotions.

Third, the empirical credentials of the view should also be questioned. When discussing the distinction between basic and nonbasic emotions, we reviewed the idea that basic emotions are often equated with so-called affect programs, i.e. specific profiles of changes along several physiological dimensions. We also saw that, although psychologists disagree about their precise number, the growing consensus is that there are a significant number of them (see Chapter 2). If that is the case, then the claim that at least some emotion types can be distinguished at the physiological level appears warranted. This of course does not speak directly against the constructionist theory and its appeal to an impoverished phenomenology, for some of those physiological changes might not rise to the level of being phenomenologically manifest. This being said, we shall see in the next chapter that many theories of the emotions – most notably that of James and those he has inspired – do precisely attempt to recruit these distinct physiological profiles to account for the felt dimension of the emotions. And this may put them in a position to distinguish on phenomenological grounds a significant number of emotion types.

All in all, then, the reversed version of the add-on theory offered by the constructionist, according to which a judgment should be added to an inchoate feeling, is perhaps plausible as an account of how in at least some complicated cases we come to know or be conscious of what emotions we are currently experiencing. As an account of the emotions themselves, however, the view is entirely unsatisfactory.

## Conclusion

As we turned our focus towards the important links existing between evaluative properties and emotions, we have in this chapter considered some theories attempting to account for the existence of these links by assimilating emotions to evaluative judgments. The evaluative judgment theory does, however, promise more than it can deliver: we saw that evaluative judgments are neither necessary nor sufficient for the emotions. Focusing on the sufficiency problem, we were then led to assess the add-on theory, according to which emotions are admixtures of evaluative judgments and phenomenological states. We offered reasons to think that the phenomenological ingredient we will have to introduce will in itself be so rich and distinctive that we can dispense with evaluative judgments altogether: the add-on theory is unmotivated and redundant. In the process we criticized, in the guise of constructionism, a reversed add-on theory, an alternative approach that conceives of the phenomenology of emotions as very impoverished. The task ahead is to better understand the nature of emotional phenomenology by considering whether there are alternative approaches to the emotions able to account for their intimate links with evaluative properties while remaining, unlike the theories reviewed in this chapter, faithful to their distinctive phenomenology. As we shall see, this is by no means an easy task.

## Questions and further readings

(1)  What sort of account of so-called irrational emotions does the evaluative judgment theory lead to?
(2)  Why say that the analysis offered by the evaluative judgment theory is not sufficient?
(3)  Why can the constructionist account be regarded as a reversed add-on theory of the emotions?

On the origins of the *evaluative judgment theory* in ancient philosophy, see Graver (2007), Nussbaum (1994) and Sorabji (2003). For thorough critical discussions of this approach, see Deigh (1994) and Roberts (2003: Chapter 1). Accounts within the framework of this theory that try to appeal to less committal attitudes than judgments are offered in Roberts (2003: 69–83), Greenspan (1988), and Neu (2000). Leighton (1984) and Stocker (1983) are good examples of criticisms of this approach, centered on the felt aspects of the emotions. Nussbaum (2004) and Solomon (2002) constitute attempts at accounting for these aspects of the emotions within the evaluative judgment theory.

For early statements of the *constructionist view* of the emotions, see Armon-Jones (1986) and Averill (1980). Bedford (1957) reaches analogous conclusions from the perspective of linguistic philosophy. For the sort of phenomenology appealed to within contemporary constructionist approaches, which tends to be conceived of in terms of the subject's reports on the valence (rating it on a scale from very negative to very positive) and arousal (rating it on a scale from low to high activation) dimensions of her experience, see Russell (2003). A presentation of Barrett's (2006) conceptual act theory and detailed criticism can be found in Deonna and Scherer (2010).

## Note

1 Some of the criticisms we shall develop may also apply to the componential process model of emotions, an influential approach to the emotions within psychology (e.g., Scherer 2009). Yet, given that many of its proponents are understandably noncommittal as regards the way the various posited components within this model (e.g., appraisal checks, subjective feelings, physiological response patterns, action tendencies) hang together (see e.g., Ellsworth and Scherer 2003), this approach as a whole remains an unwieldy target from the philosophical perspective adopted in our discussion.

# 6    Perceptual theories of the emotions

While accounting for some important aspects of the emotions, the various theories we have considered up to now face serious difficulties, which essentially have to do with the fact that they remain almost completely silent on the nature of the felt aspect of emotions. After all, one of the most surprising aspects of the evaluative judgment theory discussed in the last chapter consists in its failure to come to grips with the fact that emotions are experiences, and as such cannot be assimilated to judgments. We have thus repeatedly underlined the importance of the felt aspect of emotions and have spoken of phenomenology, qualitative experience, hedonic quality, and feeling, while leaving open the question of the relation between emotion and feeling.

The purpose of this chapter is then to gain a better grasp of the role feelings play in an analysis of emotions and to specify their nature. The starting point for our discussion will be the theory put forward by William James, a theory that identifies emotions with distinctive kinds of feelings. We shall see that this theory proves unsatisfactory, precisely because it fails to account for the intimate links between emotions and evaluative properties. This will then lead us to consider and criticize two contemporary approaches to the emotions – conceptions according to which emotions are direct or indirect perceptions of evaluative properties – that emphasize both their phenomenological aspects and their intentional relations to evaluative properties.

## James's theory

As we pointed out at the very beginning of this book, it is striking how ordinary language constantly brings to the foreground the bodily dimension of emotions. When Jonas is afraid, he feels his heart racing, his breathing quicken, his throat constrict, and so on. When Mary is ashamed, she feels the blood go to her head, her knees go weak, her shoulders fall, and so on. So why not appeal directly to these features in analyzing emotions? Descartes, for one, held that a passion is the consciousness of the activity of animal spirits in the body. This kind of view is today more commonly associated with the names of William James (1884, 1890/1950: Chapter 25) and Carl Lange (1922).

James's theory considers an emotion to be the subject's feeling of bodily modifications triggered by his apprehension of certain objects or facts. In this way, James introduces the idea that emotions consist in the subject's internal awareness of the bodily responses resulting from the interaction with her environment.

> My thesis on the contrary is that the bodily changes follow directly the PERCEPTION of the exciting fact, and that our feeling of the same changes as they occur IS the emotion.
>
> (James 1884: 189–90).

James is not only famous for this thesis, but also for the thought experiment on which he bases it, otherwise known as the subtraction argument. He tells us to imagine an emotion, and then try to abstract from our consciousness all the bodily feelings; nothing is left other than a cold and neutral intellectual state.

In positing this identity between emotions and felt bodily modifications, James places the felt aspect of emotions at center stage in his theory. The internal awareness he appeals to does undoubtedly have a qualitative dimension. From a contemporary perspective, we may say that it involves at least five underlying classes of physiological changes: facial expressions, changes in skeletal muscles, alterations in vocal expression, those of the autonomic nervous system (adrenaline and cardiac rhythm), and those changes underlying the presence of polarity or valence. Perceiving these changes from the inside constitutes what is called awareness of our peripheral responses. It is in this way that the theory places the body at the center of its analysis, a side of emotions about which the theories discussed hitherto remained surprisingly silent. Another advantage is that it is not cognitively demanding, and thus accords with the intuition that children and animals have emotions. And finally, given that the reactions of the body are not reactions of the intellect, it can easily accommodate the existence of irrational emotions, that is to say those episodes in which our feelings diverge from our evaluative judgments (see Chapter 5, pp. 54–55).

Note the following intriguing aspect of this analysis. One might think that James is putting the cart before the horse. Though it may be a bit of a caricature, is he not basically saying that we are sad because we feel our eyes well up and tears are shed, whereas common sense seems rather partisan to the reverse order of explanation: i.e. we cry because we are sad? This impression is due to the fact that we might regard the two explanations to be rival causal explanations. Yet this does not seem to be the right way to understand them. For James, the feeling of crying is constitutive of the emotion of sadness, and it is possible that the common-sense explanation ultimately refers to the same thing. The feeling of crying is a manifestation of sadness: it is not its effect, but constitutive of it.

Still, if we interpret the theory as proposing a pure and simple equivalence between emotions and perceptions of bodily changes, two significant problems crop up. First, it is not clear that all emotions are accompanied by perceptions of bodily changes. The theory seems plausible for emotions such as fear or anger, but less so for regret or hope, which can seem to be devoid of felt bodily changes. Moreover, emotions such as fear or anger, which are often accompanied by bodily sensations, can be felt very weakly, sometimes so weakly that it becomes doubtful that we feel any bodily changes at all. Still more problematic for the theory, subjects with spinal cord lesions appear to still enjoy a rich emotional life. This last problem, which has long been emphasized (Cannon 1927 and, for a recent discussion, Cobos *et al.* 2002), led to an outright rejection of the Jamesian theory: peripheral responses are simply not required for emotions.

The theory has, however, been resuscitated and modified in order to deal with this problem. The consensus today is that, though peripheral responses are not necessary, the brain regions involved in detecting bodily changes do have to be activated. It seems then that the feelings typical of certain peripheral responses can be triggered in the absence of those responses. It is as though these responses are simulated by the brain centers (Damasio *et al.* 2000, Prinz 2004: 58–59). Some evidence suggests that this kind of 'short-cut' (bypassing the body) taken by the brain centers is precisely what is involved when we simulate emotions, as when we gauge through imagination how we would feel in certain circumstances, or empathize with others by putting ourselves in their shoes. Were this hypothesis to be confirmed, it would do much to salvage theories of emotions along these Jamesian lines. An emotion would then either consist in the veridical perception of certain bodily changes or, when such changes are not present, in the simulation of such perception. Note that this explanation still requires that all emotions involve a certain bodily feeling, and so amounts to rejecting the intuition that certain emotions such as hope and regret do not have them.

Second, it is not clear that this internal perception is sufficient to identify emotions. If emotions are nothing but bodily feelings, each emotion type must be distinguishable in terms of the feelings peculiar to it. And yet it is unclear whether bodily feelings are as emotion-specific as the theory requires. For instance, what are the differences at this level between joy and pride? These issues must be resolved empirically, and the current evidence is not unfavorable to the idea that it is possible to individuate in this manner at least a significant number of emotions – those that are commonly thought of as basic (see Chapter 2). Contemporary theories that share the fundamental Jamesian insight regarding the role of bodily feelings in emotions, like the theory of Prinz we shall shortly present and the one we shall defend in Chapter 7, must build on this optimism.

But the problem of the sufficiency of bodily sensations arises in another more serious form, which reveals what has been traditionally perceived as a fundamental flaw in James's account. Indeed, it seems that the bodily changes that one perceives, say, when falling ill, can be very similar to those one perceives in the course of an episode of disgust directed at a cream cake. Yet there is a fundamental difference between these two cases. As we have already stressed, an emotion like disgust is not experienced by us – at least not directly – as a state directed at our own body. On the contrary, disgust is directed at an object that we experience as disgusting, an insight that lies at the heart of the evaluative judgment theory. This very phenomenon, so clearly incompatible with the idea that an emotion is nothing but a perception of the changes in our own body, is enough to reject this model, and is the principal motivation behind contemporary theories that seek to reconcile, in one way or another, the thought that emotions are distinctive modes of apprehending salient features of the environment with the thought that they are essentially felt.

## Emotions as direct perceptions of values

Before we introduce these contemporary theories, let us first recall the central idea of the evaluative judgment theory. Beyond its effects on our body, the principal feature of an emotion is to inform the subject of the significance objects and events have for her. Emotions reveal to us a world imbued with value. We need in one way or another to account both for this informational function and for the felt aspect of emotions. We have seen that on the one side we run into problems if we are to account for this informational aspect of emotions in terms of fully fledged evaluative *judgments* (or even thoughts or construals), on the other side reducing emotion to pure feeling ends up silently discounting this informational aspect.

   This leaves us casting about for some way of uniting these two features within a single model. (Thinking of emotional experiences on the model of perceptual experiences might be the way forward.) For the philosophy of perception has, after having tried to analyze perceptual phenomena by iden-tifying them with propositional attitudes like judgments (Armstrong 1968, Pitcher 1971), more recently endeavored to bring out their specificity. The intentionality of perception is often considered as irreducible to judgment for at least three reasons. First, perception has a phenomenology that cannot be captured by a simple appeal to judgment. Having a visual experience of a blue vase has a feel that the corresponding judgment does not have (Goldman 1976). Second, perception does not necessarily require the exercise of the concepts used to represent its content: seeing a blue vase does not require the mastery of the concepts of blue or vase (Crane 1992). Third, perception generally allows for more fine-grained discriminations of content than the associated judgments. We can visually discriminate thousands of shades of color for which we simply lack the corresponding concepts (e.g., Dretske 1981: 135–53). And these same features seem to be equally true of emotions: we have more than once insisted on their phenomenology and have argued that evaluative judgments fail to capture its richness. We have also insisted on the fact that creatures devoid of evaluative concepts can nevertheless experience emotions, and we may surmise that the sensitivity to evaluative properties that they authorize is more fine-grained than the discriminations that evaluative judgments provide for. The idea would be, for instance, that the intensity of one's fear co-varies with the degree of danger one faces, something our comparatively coarse evaluative judgments may prove unable to capture.

Hence the idea that emotions are not judgments but *perceptions* of values (e.g., de Sousa 1987 and Tappolet 2000). Being afraid is to perceive danger, being sad is to perceive a loss, much as having a visual perceptual experience is to perceive, say, a red circle. To an adherent of this theory, we do not need to deploy the concepts of danger or loss in order to experience, respectively, fear and sadness, any more than we need to deploy the concept of a red circle to see one. The territory we have covered thus far allows us to see the merits of this analysis.

First of all, emotions are assigned the same mind-to-world direction of fit as judgments without being assimilated to them. In this way the analysis satisfies the intuition that emotions play an important *intentional role* in revealing to us a world of values. The analysis can accordingly individuate the emotion types by means of the specific values that each reveals. It also does it in a manner that respects an important intuition about the *phenomenological role* of emotions: emotions are a form of affective perception through which a world of evaluative properties is presented to us in an experientially salient way. Finally, this analysis becomes especially attractive when one sees that the relation between emotions and evaluative judgments seems analogous to that between perceptual experiences and perceptual judgments. In the same way as one is tempted to say that perceptual experiences cause and justify the associated judgments, emotions seem also to cause and justify evaluative judgments. The general idea is that our emotions, because they are experiences of values, have the potential to become reasons for the relevant evaluative judgments – and it might be thought that this is their distinctive *epistemological role*. For instance, Jonas's anger at a given remark provides him with a defeasible reason for believing the remark is offensive. That is to say that in the absence of any countervailing reason, his belief is justified in the light of his anger. What is more, if emotions as perceptions of evaluative properties are conceived as potential reasons for the corresponding evaluative judgments, the present suggestion also explains the cases of irrational emotions, which were so problematic for the evaluative judgment theory, by likening them to perceptual illusions: phobias can be regarded as forms of affective illusions. Just as one can without contradiction see the two lines in the Müller-Lyer illusion as having different lengths while knowing that they are of the same length, one can also without inconsistency fear a little spider while fully aware that it is harmless (Tappolet 2000, Döring 2009).

Although the perceptual theory of emotion seems particularly well suited to account for the specific intentional, phenomenological, and epistemological roles of the emotions, it promises perhaps more than it can deliver. How is one to understand the appeal to perception? Is it simply an analogy, or should one take this idea of evaluative perception literally? If the perceptual model is understood in the literal sense, what model are we appealing to?

Strictly speaking, after all, perception is associated with certain sensory modalities and specific organs. This may be a reason – although clearly not a conclusive reason (see Prinz 2004: Chapter 10) – to think that the perceptual model cannot be applied literally, since there is no organ of emotion that is capable of playing the same role as the eye or the ear. As enticing as the proposal may be, we shall now see that one can list as many fundamental dissimilarities as one can similarities between the two kinds of phenomena.

The first point to emphasize is that the proposal flies in the face of ordinary language given the way we talk about the emotions. The perceptual model has it that emotions are literally about values, in exactly the same way as an object's color and shape are what a given visual experience is about. It is thus revisionary with respect to everyday talk about emotions, since we would not ordinarily say that we are afraid of danger or angry at the offensive (unless, perhaps, we were explaining the meaning of these words to someone), but rather that we are afraid of the lion and angry at a given person. Putting aside this linguistic remark, to which we shall return later on (see Chapter 7), let us consider some further important dissimilarities between perceptions and emotions. For one thing, is it not strange to hold that, like perceptions, emotions are mere detection mechanisms for certain kinds of information, when we know that, unlike perceptions, they are highly dependent on the subject's motivations, beliefs, and character traits? Sam's experiencing George's funny remark as crass is, say, directly informed by his snobbery. For another, as already noted, the content of a perception is answerable to a causal constraint: the perceived objects and properties have to be causally responsible for the occurrence of the perceptual experience. Sam perceives the redness of this tomato only if this tomato and its redness cause his visual experience, and he only *seems* to perceive them when such a constraint is not fulfilled. Of course, this does not seem true in the case of the emotions. Sam may really feel afraid of a non-existent spider he has just imagined, and we do not simply *seem* to undergo an emotion when it turns out that the object it is directed at does not exemplify the relevant evaluative property.

Even assuming that these difficulties can be overcome, the phenomenology of emotions that motivates the analogy is not easy to assimilate to the phenomenology of perception, for at least two reasons. First, many, perhaps all, emotions are said to be essentially valenced experiences (an emotion is either positive or negative), whereas we tend to think of perceptions as not being essentially so – although they may of course become positive or negative when colored by affective phenomena. Second, perceptual experiences are what is in philosophical parlance called 'transparent' (Harman 1990). Try, for instance, to describe the content of the visual experience of a vase of flowers on a table. You will realize that it is very difficult to mention anything other than the properties exemplified by the objects that you see; the vase has such and such a nuance of blue, the flowers have this or that form, color, and texture. All these elements are given to us as the properties of the perceived object and not as properties of the perceptual experience, and this is why these experiences are said to be transparent. Yet this is not so obviously the case for emotional experience. One could argue that the felt quality of fear is not clearly experienced by us as a feature of the spider that frightens us, nor is that of gratitude given as a property of such and such a benefactor. If you are to describe how it feels to be frightened by a spider, you would not do so in terms of the spider's qualities, but rather in terms of how it feels to experience a jolt up your spine, your hair standing on end, your teeth clenching, muscles freezing, heart jumping, etc. And these felt changes in your body are definitely not what you apprehend as dangerous in the circumstances (but see Soldati 2008 and Tye 2008). In assimilating emotion to perception, the perceptual model is thus papering over some crucial phenomenological differences, insofar as it remains silent on which aspect of the complex phenomenology of emotions is apt to play the role of perceptually presenting evaluative properties.

Let us finally set out what in our eyes constitutes the most serious objection to a perceptual analysis. Even if emotions are to be seen as independent or *sui generis* ways of accessing the evaluative properties that they reveal, they differ from perceptions in that they cannot be seen as independent ways of accessing the objects that exemplify these properties. For instance, while the injustice of Jonas's remark is perceived by Mary through her indignation, the remark itself is not. Mary must access it by some other means (perception, memory, belief, etc.), which as such constitute what we have called in Chapter 1 the cognitive base of her indignation; she hears the remark and feels it is unjust. The evaluative apprehension at the heart of the perceptual theory is grounded in such non-evaluative bases: they cause and, in a sense yet to be clarified, explain the occurrence of emotions. And, as is perhaps too obvious to mention, there is no such comparable distinction between two psychological levels exemplifying causal and epistemic relations within the field of perception proper.

The existence of such cognitive bases for emotions raises doubt regarding the epistemological role the perceptual model accords emotions. For the epistemological status we assign emotions in our everyday life is not easy to reconcile with the perceptualist's way of conceiving them. Indeed, there is a sort of *why-question* we typically ask with respect to the emotions, which we have not the slightest inclination to ask with respect to perceptions. We perhaps could ask someone: 'Why do you see that tree?' But in so doing we would not be asking about the reasons he has for his perceptual experience, at least not in the sense in which we do ask for such reasons when we ask: 'Why are you afraid of the dog?' What this suggests is that, contrary to the epistemological picture fostered by the perceptual model, emotions should not primarily be thought of as states that provide us with reasons for anything, but rather as states for which reasons are needed (Brady 2010). This issue will be at the center of our discussions from Chapter 8 onwards.

At this stage, we may start to wonder whether the very plausibility of the perceptual model is not entirely derived from an undue focus on the small, and not necessarily representative, class of emotions that are based on perceptual experiences of the relevant object. While it may make sense to say that one is in a perceptual relation with the relevant evaluative properties when the object is perceptually present, it hardly does so when the only access one has to the object is through, say, testimony. In what sense is one in perceptual contact with the offensiveness of a certain remark when we know of it through a third party 10 years after the fact?

Something like the worries just presented may provide reason to take the appeal to the perceptual model as a mere analogy, which amounts to high-lighting, as we have done above, a certain number of similarities between emotions and perceptual experiences. We may describe this as the relaxed perceptual model. This is, for instance, the best way of understanding Linda Zagzebski's appeal to 'affective perceptions of values' (Zagzebski 2003) or Peter Goldie's 'feelings towards', which he places at the heart of his theory of emotions (Goldie 2000: Chapter 3). The latter idea is that, to cleave closely to the phenomenology of emotions, one must introduce an experiential ele-ment directed towards the object of one's emotion. And here the introduction of 'feelings towards' does not imply that these experiences are the only con-stituents of emotions; they will typically encompass this along with a host of other elements, amongst them certain bodily feelings. The crucial point, as Goldie insists, is that the 'feelings towards' do not constitute an extra layer on top of affective experience proper (see the discussion of add-on theories in Chapter 5); it is not an extraneous addition, but in fact the way in which the world is evaluatively presented to us through emotions.

The theory of 'feelings towards' is certainly attractive. It specifies perfectly what one demands of an adequate account of the emotions. Yet, although something along the lines of 'feelings towards' is required by the analysis, it seems that this expression is as it stands a mere placeholder for *whatever adequately fulfills the function of making the subject experientially aware of evaluative properties.* But to leave matters in this state is to expose one's flank to the recurrent line of attack that intuitionism about evaluative properties has always been vulnerable to. For, after all, what is a 'feeling towards'? Empirical affective science does not help us on this point.

This discussion of the perceptual model, in its literal or in its more relaxed form, brings out the fact that the perceptual metaphor does not so much advance the ball as hide it. And the metaphor is more misleading than it seems; in fact there needs to be a clear distinction between perception on the one hand and emotion on the other, in order to be able to articulate the relevant relations between emotions and their various cognitive bases. Now, all this should not make us conclude that the reasons motivating the perceptual model are misplaced, but rather that they should be understood in a manner that can accommodate the specificities of emotional experiences. If, first, emotions do indeed stand in intentional relations to values, they must do so in a way that will also satisfy the idea that emotions are typically not about these values but about their bearers (this is what we shall henceforth call the *intentionality constraint*). If, second, a satisfactory account endorses the view that it is through emotional phenomenology that the evaluative aspects of the world are made manifest to us, it should not do so by positing a mysterious perceptual or quasi-perceptual relation to values (*phenomenology constraint*). Third, if emotions are privileged – even perhaps indispensable – sources of justification for evaluative judgments, this should not make us forget that emotions essentially depend on the fact that other cognitive states provide them with their objects (*epistemological constraint*).

## Emotions as indirect perceptions of values

The direct perception model as we presented it is promising but too fragmentary. We still face the task of finding a way to combine the phenomenological, intentional, and epistemological roles of emotions in a satisfactory manner. Laying aside any radical alternatives to the family of theories just examined, the solution must in our view reconcile the Jamesian intuition that the body is essential to emotions with the idea that they have an intrinsic evaluative intentionality. In short, the key challenge concerns how to make sense of the idea that the only kind of phenomenology clearly admitted both by the empirical affective sciences and by the first-person perspective, which is to say that of the felt body, can put us in relation with evaluative properties.

James says that emotions are perceptions of bodily changes. One might at this point inquire into the occasions or situations in which different types of such changes – and thereby the attendant perception – occur. One might surmise that different types of bodily changes correspond to different types of situations encountered by the subject. The idea would then be that there is a systematic co-variation between the perception of certain types of situations and the triggering of bodily changes. For instance, the perception of snakes or spiders systematically triggers the bodily changes associated with fear. Equally, perhaps not in an innate but an acquired manner, the perceptions of one's moral wrongdoing systematically trigger the bodily changes associated with shame.

According to a view popular amongst contemporary philosophers, such co-variations constitute the heart of an analysis of intentionality (Dretske 1981). Why? Fire causes smoke, heat causes a strip of mercury to rise, chicken pox causes skin lesions. A philosopher with naturalistic proclivities will be tempted to exploit the existence of such causal co-variations to analyze the notion of intentionality. For, if fire causes smoke, it follows that smoke indicates the presence of fire; it then becomes attractive to conceive of these relations of indication as the basis of a possible representational function. If something co-varies with something else because it was *designed* or *meant* to do so, either through the intentions of someone (e.g., rise of mercury and temperature) or through evolutionary pressures (e.g., pain and tissue damage), it makes sense to say that the former is not only an indication of the latter but represents it because it has the relevant function (Millikan 1987). Thus one might maintain that, since some bodily changes co-vary in the same way with certain types of situations, the first have the *function* of representing the latter. If the bodily changes typical of fear have been selected by evolution to co-vary with some property common to various types of situations eliciting them, because detection of this common property is relevant for the organism's biological fitness, then these bodily changes might be said to represent this property. And do these typical situations not precisely exemplify what we have called the formal object of emotions, in this case danger? One could then conclude that the subject's perception of some bodily changes associated with fear constitutes also a representation of the danger that he faces.

This neo-Jamesian theory, the most detailed version of which has been developed by Prinz (2004), proposes an original way of combining the three fundamental roles of emotions highlighted in the previous section. Their felt quality, identified here under the influence of James with bodily feelings, is equally the bearer of intentionality: the bodily feelings have the function of representing evaluative properties. What is more, this theory provides an account of the relation between emotions and their cognitive bases as well as, potentially, an account of the relation between the emotions and the evaluative judgments that they may ground. Awareness of bodily changes is caused and potentially justified by distinct cognitive bases – whether they be perceptions, memories, or complex testimonies. And awareness of the relevant bodily changes might in turn constitute one's reason to make a given evaluative judgment. The theory is thus ingenious and appealing in the way it combines our three constraints.

Within this theory, the relation between emotions and evaluative properties is conceived of as a particular instance of the relation between elements connected by causal co-variation. But is such a relation between bodily disturbances and evaluative properties capable of accounting for the representational relation between emotions and evaluative properties? On its face, it would not seem that such a relation is the kind of intentional relation from a first-person perspective that an advocate of the perceptual model or the evaluative judg-ment theory had in mind when casting about for an explanation of the way evaluative properties are given to us through emotions. However, perhaps we are going too fast: after all, the theory holds that it is perception or awareness of bodily disturbances, that is to say something that is truly a first-person intentional act, and not the disturbances themselves, which serves to explain the representational relation between emotions and evaluative properties. Can we then appeal to this relation to elucidate the specific evaluative intentionality of emotions? We can at any rate say for instance that, just as the perceptual appearance of water constitutes an intentional relation to what turns out to be $H_2O$, the awareness of certain changes in our body constitutes an intentional relation to this or that evaluative property (Prinz 2004: 67–69). But, apart from any sympathy that one may or may not have for such a program of naturalizing intentionality, this much is clear: though it makes sense to claim that $H_2O$ is given to us through the appearance of water, it is not perceptually given to us under the aspect of $H_2O$. Yet is danger not given to us through fear precisely as *danger*, in the sense that the phenomenology of fear is what makes this evaluative aspect of the world manifest to us? This idea is at least at the center of those theories that conceive of emotions as cognitions of evaluative properties and what lends them their intuitive appeal.

However one wants to answer this last question, the difficulty is compounded for emotions as the neo-Jamesian theory conceives them. For, if the bodily sensations are thought of as fully fledged perceptions, i.e. as intentional acts that have as their object certain parts of the body, then the analogy with the case of perception of water falls apart. In the latter case, there are not two distinct candidates for the status of object of the perceptual awareness: $H_2O$ and whatever is visually given to us. There is only one, since the relation between $H_2O$ and the watery stuff we see is one of identity or constitution. By contrast, when we are dealing with the bodily feelings enlisted by the neo-Jamesian theory to function as the apprehension of evaluative properties, there seems to be a real competition between two distinct objects. Bodily feelings already have an intentional object: those parts of the body that we feel in some particular way. And the relation between the felt parts of the body and the evaluative property is clearly not one of constitution. It is obviously not the case that the evaluative property is to the felt parts of the body what $H_2O$ is to the properties manifested in visual perception of water. In this sense, there is really no intentional relation to the value, whether it be perceptual or judicative. This is also why adherents of this theory must consider as a possible addition – though not one necessary to the occurrence of an emotion – an intentional relation to the value that takes the form of an evaluative judgment. One finds here again the reversed form of the add-on strategy exemplified by constructionist theories discussed in Chapter 4, which consists in adding a judgment to an experience that does not in itself constitute an intentional access to evaluative properties. We are now indeed tempted to describe the present option in exactly the same terms.

It is also worth unpacking the epistemological implications of the neo-Jamesian theory. The worry here relates to the fact that, while the theory is in a position to articulate and make sense of the epistemological relations existing between emotions and their cognitive bases, it may not be able to make sense of the relations between emotions and evaluative judgments. Recall that an alleged virtue of the perceptual model consists in leveraging the apparent parallel relations between perceptions and perceptual judgments, on the one hand, and emotions and evaluative judgments, on the other. In both cases, the idea is that a certain experiential access to a kind of information causes and potentially justifies the forming of a judgment. Yet on the view under consideration, the parallel gets bent out of shape. This is the case because, as you will recall, the 'perception of evaluative properties' is in the present case indirect at best – we become aware of the presence of evaluative properties by inference through our awareness of bodily changes, much like we become aware of the presence of fire when we see smoke. This of course is not to deny that the theory can

admit the existence of a more indirect relation between emotions and evaluative judgments. A practiced observer may well be able to infer the presence of
a certain evaluative property by having learned to take his bodily sensations
as a sign of a certain kind of co-varying feature of his surroundings, and on
this basis come to the relevant evaluative judgment. However, if we can
perhaps in this way recover part of the parallel with perceptual judgments,
we have in the process lost one of its crucial features. Our practiced observer
must not only be able to associate what she is currently feeling with what she
knows to be the co-varying evaluative property, but she must also attach this
property to the relevant feature of the emotion's cognitive base, for instance a
particular element of a complex scene that she sees. That is to say, it is still
up to the observer to accomplish the important task of establishing the connection between the evaluative properties and the perceived objects as the
connection is not accessible through the emotion (see Prinz 2005).

Now, although we are at times in the position of having to reflect on what
it is that make us feel the way we do – as you will recall, this is what the
constructionist does not tire of emphasizing (see Chapter 4) – there is no
reason to think that this subset of cases captures the typical epistemological
situation we are in when we feel emotions. The situation is generally not one
in which we tell ourselves something along the lines of: 'there is something
going on within me I know to be indicative of danger, loss, offense, etc., but
where is it exactly located in my surroundings?' Note that the lesson to be
drawn from the present discussion is quite general. For, even if the epistemological status of evaluative judgments ultimately had nothing to do with
the emotions, i.e. if emotional experiences played no fundamental role in our
knowledge of values, an adequate theory of emotions must still cover the fact
that we often make evaluative judgments because of the emotions we experience.
And the way in which the present approach forces us to articulate this relation –
to wit, as an intellectual and indirect access to evaluative properties – is at
variance with the usual way in which these judgments are formed.

## Conclusion

We considered here in some detail theories that take seriously the idea that
emotions are essentially felt. After having criticized James's theory on account
of it failing to meet what we called the intentionality constraint, we were led
to present and assess perceptual models of the emotions according to which
emotions are either direct or indirect perceptions of evaluative properties. We
argued that the model of direct perception has, when interpreted literally,
little to recommend itself, and that its more relaxed form looks more like a
promise of a theory than a theory. This conclusion prompted us to consider
the idea that emotions are indirect perceptions of evaluative properties. Such
an approach, in the form of the neo-Jamesian theory, however, does not suc-
cessfully combine the phenomenological, intentional, and epistemological
constraints weighing on a satisfactory account of the emotions. In particular,

it cannot do justice to the idea that the dangerousness of the lion is given to us in the experience of its predatory posture (we experience it as dangerous), or that the majesty of this cathedral is given to us in the experience of its facade (we experience it as majestic).

Nonetheless, at this stage we should not be tempted to draw the conclusion that the phenomenology of bodily feeling is not up to the task of accounting for the evaluative intentionality of emotion, and that we should look to some other form of phenomenology to fulfill this role. Going down this path merely leads us back to the previously discussed problems attending the perceptual theories.

## Questions and further readings

(1)  What are the main problems faced by the Jamesian theory of the emotions?
(2)  Are emotions perceptions?
(3)  How do bodily feelings come to represent evaluative properties in Prinz's theory?

Ratcliffe (2005) and Ellsworth (1994) provide reasons for thinking that *William James* gives more attention to the world directedness of the emotions than is usually claimed. Damasio (2000) does for psychology what Prinz (2004) does for philosophy, i.e. he reconciles cognitive and feeling theories of the emotions within a Jamesian framework.

The perceptual analogy is nicely drawn in de Sousa (1987: 149–58). Aside from Goldie (2000: Chapter 3) and Tappolet (2000), recent sympathizers of a *perceptual approach* to the emotions are Deonna (2006), Döring (2007), Johnston (2001), and Tye (2008). Goldie (2009) persuasively stresses the role of feeling in accounting for the emotions' world directedness. While Deonna (2006) attempts to downplay some of the dissimilarities between emotions and perceptions, Brady (2010), Salmela (2011), Wedgwood (2001), and Whiting (2012) adopt for various reasons a resolutely skeptical attitude towards the approach.

# 7 The attitudinal theory of emotions

In the previous chapter, we saw that, despite its sound motivations and initial promise, the perceptual approach to the emotions fails to convince. Our discussion helped, however, to sharpen the formulation of some basic intentional, phenomenological, and epistemological constraints that any satisfactory theory of the emotions must respect. In this chapter, we defend a theory of the emotions that we believe can meet these constraints satisfactorily. According to this attitudinal theory, an emotion is an attitude towards an object, an attitude which it is appropriate to have when the latter exemplifies a given evaluative property. After introducing the contrast between attitudes and content, we argue that the relation between emotions and evaluative properties is best elucidated by conceiving of the different emotions as distinctive evaluative attitudes as opposed to attitudes directed towards evaluative contents. We then give substance to the claim that emotions are attitudes by elaborating on the idea that they consist in specific types of felt bodily stances directed towards objects. In the final section, we show how the attitudinal theory allows us to meet the phenomenological and intentional constraints in an appealing way, leaving the question of how the resources of the theory can be deployed in meeting the epistemological constraint for the next three chapters.

## Attitudes and contents

As we noted, values are said to be the formal objects of the emotions. What does that mean? Truth is said to be the formal object of belief; to believe is to take a proposition to be true. The 'oughtness' of a state of affairs is often said to be the formal object of desire; to desire is to regard a state of affairs as something that ought to obtain. Possibility may be held to be the formal object of supposition; to suppose is to take a state of affairs to be possible. And perhaps probability can be claimed to be the formal object of conjecture; to conjecture is to take a state of affairs to be probable.

These illustrations allow us to see the role formal objects play in a theory of mental phenomena: they individuate the relevant *type* of mental state. Since a belief, a desire, a supposition, and a conjecture can be about the same state of affairs, we have the basis for a very natural distinction between attitudes on the one hand and what attitudes are directed at (their object or content) on the other.[1] Furthermore, attitude and content are both understood as making essential contributions to the distinctive nature of mental states by jointly determining the correctness conditions of a given instance of a type of mental state. For example, it is because Sam adopts the attitude of belief towards P that the correctness condition of his mental state is the truth of P; the correctness condition would be the truth of Q were he to take this attitude towards Q; and it would be the probability of P were he to adopt the attitude of conjecture towards it.

Now, the way we ordinarily speak motivates the application of this central distinction to the emotions. We shall for that reason make use of the idea, often expressed but not really followed through on when philosophers introduce basic distinctions in the philosophy of mind (e.g., Searle 1983: Chapter 1, Crane 2001: Chapter 1), that an emotion is an attitude we take towards a specific object or content. In fearing the dog, we have an attitude towards the dog; in being angry at John, we have an attitude towards him. And, in both instances, the correctness conditions of the mental state are determined by the respective contributions of the attitude and content in question. If we now take the idea of evaluative properties as the formal objects of emotions at face value (danger in the case of fear, offensiveness in the case of anger), this appears to imply, given the other examples of attitudes we have considered, that the fact that emotions have evaluative properties amongst their correctness conditions traces back to the fact that they are specific attitudes – namely evaluative attitudes – and not to the fact that they have a specific content. Let us motivate and clarify this claim.

If it makes sense to say that what frightens Julianne is what John is amused by – a dog, for instance – then we have reason enough to think that the difference between their two emotions is not to be located at the level of their respective contents. If this difference were located at the level of the content, that would imply that Julianne is frightened by (a specific instance of) dangerousness, whereas John is amused by (a specific instance of) funniness; their respective emotions would then be about different things. The contrast here is analogous to that between attitude and content in the case of other mental states. Consider belief. If it makes sense to say that what John believes is what Julianne doubts, then the reason why truth enters only into the correctness conditions of John's mental state has to do with the fact that only he takes the specific attitude of belief towards it. Similarly, it is because one adopts a specific emotional attitude towards a given object that the corresponding evaluative property becomes relevant for determining whether this emotion is correct or not. It is for instance because Julianne takes the attitude of fear towards the dog that its dangerousness features in the correctness conditions of her mental state.

This way of articulating the structure of an emotional episode not only guarantees the possibility of sameness of content across different attitudes, but it is also and unsurprisingly consistent with everyday talk involving emotions and what they are about. In the present framework, what we have called the particular objects of the emotions (Chapter 1, p. 5) are the (potential or actual) bearers of evaluative properties, and not the evaluative properties themselves. To put this in the language we have used from Chapter 1 onwards, emotions are about the particular objects that are provided by the various psychological states that function as their cognitive bases: they are attitudes that we take towards these objects. And this is good news, since it accords with our ordinary way of talking about the emotions and thus avoids the revisionary implications of the perceptual model, according to which evaluative properties end up being what the emotions are about.

But this of course leads us to the following important question: if the relation with evaluative properties cannot be handled by having them figure in the content of the emotions, but has rather to do with their being specific attitudes, how exactly are we to understand emotions conceived as evaluative attitudes?

## Emotions as felt bodily attitudes

A preliminary issue concerns whether the various emotional attitudes are determinates of one more general determinable emotional attitude. One option would be to say that this general attitude consists in emoting, i.e. in taking something as (dis)valuable. While this might constitute a way of abstractly describing what emotional attitudes are, there is no reason to think that this general attitude, emoting, has any psychological reality over and above that of its determinate instances, i.e. the distinct and specific emotional attitudes one may have. For that reason, our claim shall be that, to each type of emotion, there corresponds a distinct type of evaluative attitude.

In order to better understand the claim that emotions are distinctive evaluative attitudes, it is helpful to appreciate that we can draw several distinctions within the general category of attitudes. Amongst attitudes, we can distinguish propositional from non-propositional attitudes. Propositional attitudes take propositions as their objects, as when one believes or surmises that P. Examples of non-propositional attitudes are episodic memory (Luke remembers his first meeting with Lucy) and sensory imagining (Michelle imagines a pink elephant). While it has been common philosophical practice to try to analyse non-propositional attitudes in terms of propositional ones, the idea that there are irreducibly non-propositional attitudes has recently received much attention and increased support (e.g., Crane 2007, Montague 2007). Another important distinction amongst attitudes is that between occurrent and dispositional ones. You may believe that the Earth is round in the sense that you are disposed to assert this proposition, to use it in arguments, to be baffled by those who think otherwise, etc. Alternatively, you have an occurrent attitude of, say, supposing a given proposition to be the case when you are actively thinking through its implications. Amongst both dispositional and occurrent attitudes, but more obviously amongst the latter, we can further distinguish those that have salient phenomenological aspects from those that have a less salient phenomenology, or maybe no phenomenology at all, i.e. we can distinguish between experiential and non-experiential attitudes. Some think for instance that while occurrently believing that P has no phenomenology at all (Julianne believes that it is just before noon), there is a distinctive phenomenology in propositional remembering (John seems to remember that Moscow is the capital of Russia) (e.g., Audi 1995). We do not have to enter into these difficult issues for our present purposes. Indeed, while for most attitudes it appears difficult to provide a substantive psychological description of what they are, this may prove more straightforward for emotions, or at least for many of them, as we shall see.

As a first step in this direction, let us now see how the aforementioned distinctions amongst attitudes may help us home in on the sorts of attitudes emotions are. There is, it is true, no a priori reason to think that, because all the different emotional attitudes contribute to the mental state having the evaluative correctness conditions it has, all of them must for that reason be psychologically realized in the same way. This is not to say that there are no constraints on what emotional attitudes could be, however. For, while the structure of the present proposal allows us in principle to cash out the attitude component in many different ways, our survey of the various theories of the emotions has revealed that any complete account must be informed by the following facts. Emotions are often not directed at propositions, they are episodes, they have a salient experiential dimension, their phenomenology is best captured in terms of bodily feelings, and it is in virtue of their phenomenology that emotions relate to evaluative properties. All of which raises the question: how do these facts constrain an account of the psychological nature of emotions understood as experiential evaluative attitudes?

We can answer this question, we suggest, by elaborating on the idea that the emotionally relevant bodily changes are experienced as distinct stances we adopt towards specific objects. That is to say, we should conceive of emotions as distinctive types of bodily awareness, where the subject experiences her body holistically as taking an attitude towards a certain object, or, as Edouard Claparède, an early eloquent advocate of such a view, writes while building on William James's insight, there is a 'consciousness of a form, of a "Gestalt", of these multiple organic impressions [bodily feelings] [ ... ] the consciousness of a global attitude of the organism' (Claparède 1928: 128). The key idea, then, is to move away from the curiously atomistic approach to bodily sensations implicit in many accounts of their role in emotions and recognize that, in emotions, these sensations are typically aspects of a whole pattern that constitutes a world-directed attitude. And it is possible to go quite far in developing this proposal by appealing to an idea that is common currency in the psychological literature on the emotions, namely the idea that emotions are intimately connected with types of action readiness or, more precisely, felt action readiness. Feelings of action readiness are indeed obvious candidates for elucidating the nature of emotions as involving awareness of one's body adopting a specific stance towards an object or being poised to act in given ways in relation to an object, one that sheds light on the idea that emotions make us apprehend the world in evaluative terms. Frijda, when describing the world-focused dimension of emotional experiences, speaks in expressive if sometimes figurative terms of the contribution of action readiness in imbuing the world with significance:

> Action readiness transforms a neutral world into one with places of danger and openings towards safety, in fear, with targets for kissing and their being accessible for it, in enamoration, with roads stretching out endlessly before one, in fatigue, misery, and despair, with insistent calls for entry or participation or consumption, in enjoyment.
>
> (Frijda 2007: 205).

This illustrates the manner in which states of action readiness, at any rate when they are felt, contribute essentially to the world being presented to the subject as significant for her in various ways.[2] The idea driving the present proposal, then, is the following: we give substance to the claim that emotions constitute evaluative attitudes when we realize that they are such attitudes in virtue of being experiences of our body as ready or poised to act in various ways towards an object. And to prevent a misunderstanding this formulation may invite, let us emphasize that the proposal is not that emotions are attitudes we take towards what we feel happens in our body, but that what we feel happens in our body constitutes in itself an emotional attitude. Emotions are not attitudes we take towards our felt body, but felt bodily attitudes directed towards the world.

This being clarified, the notion of action readiness we here appeal to should be conceived in quite an inclusive manner, for it must not only cover aspects such as the tendency to move away, towards or against a given object, but also the tendency to attend to an object, to submit or to be drawn to it, to disengage from it, or even to suspend any inclination to interact with it, and so on. Consider the following examples by way of illustration. In fear, the relevant action readiness should be described as follows: we feel the way our body is poised to act in a way that will contribute to the neutralization of what provokes the fear. In anger, we feel the way our body is prepared for active hostility to whatever causes the anger. In shame, we feel the way our body is poised to hide from the gaze of others that typically causes the shame. In an episode of loving affection, we feel the way our body is prepared to move towards cuddling the object of one's affection. In disgust, we feel the way our body is poised to prevent the object from entering into contact with it. And in sadness, our body is given to us as though prevented from entering into interaction with a certain object. These descriptions, meant to capture the holistic felt bodily attitudes characteristic of the emotions, refer to experiences that integrate information coming from a variety of sources, such as facial feedback, changes in skeletal muscles, as well as those of the autonomic nervous system (e.g., heart rate, perspiration, respiration, digestion, etc.) and the endocrine system (e.g., adrenaline). It is, we submit, because emotions are, unlike beliefs and desires for instance, attitudes that lend themselves to such rich descriptions and give rise to such interesting generalizations that being told someone is afraid or angry – without any further specification of what he is afraid of or angry at – is already informative, an observation we made at the very beginning of this book.

Now, in what sense do these states of felt action readiness make the emotions *evaluative* attitudes? To put it differently, how do distinct felt bodily stances help account for the fact that distinct emotions are correct only when their object exemplifies a specific evaluative property? The answer is both straightforward and illuminating. Fear of the dog is an experience of the dog as dangerous, precisely because it consists in feeling the body's readiness to act so as to diminish the dog's likely impact on it (flight, preemptive attack, etc.), and this felt attitude is correct if and only if the dog is dangerous. Similarly, anger at someone is an experience of her as offensive, precisely because it consists in feeling the body's readiness to act so as to retaliate one way or another, and this felt attitude is correct if and only if the person is or has been offensive. Shame of oneself is an experience of oneself as degraded, precisely because it consists in feeling one's body ready to act so as to disappear into the ground or perhaps from the view of others, and this felt attitude is correct if and only if the person is degraded. Admiration is an experience of a given object as admirable, because it consists in feeling the way one's body opens up to sustained and expanding exploration of the object, and it is correct if and only if the object is admirable.

We have just illustrated with a few examples how the approach we recommend should be pursued. Its fruitfulness depends of course on the possibility of providing substantial and convincing characterizations in terms of felt bodily attitudes for all emotions. At this stage, two observations are in order. First, our approach, like that of James, treats bodily feelings as constitutive of the emotions and not as consequences of them. Yet, we believe that our version of the attitudinal theory is not subject to the same difficulties (Chapter 6, pp. 65–66). For the felt bodily stances the attitudinal theory appeals to illuminate the sense in which the emotions are directed towards the world. Second, we should emphasize that while the present account must conceive of the emotions as stances or postures we take towards objects, these attitudes need not be bodily attitudes. Those skeptical of the possibility of coming up with such informative characterizations for some emotions – regret? pride? – might still embrace the above framework and try to account for these alleg-edly recalcitrant emotions in terms of felt, yet non-embodied, attitudes. That is to say, the overall architecture of the theory perhaps offers a flexibility that is not shared by Jamesian or neo-Jamesian alternatives. In our opinion, though, the journey completed thus far should make us question the viability of a non-embodied account of the emotions and should rather be viewed as supporting optimism regarding the prospects of understanding the emotions in the terms we recommend. So, we think, do the ramifications and virtues of this approach we shall now explore in connection with many of the issues we have already had occasion to touch upon.

## Virtues of the theory

For starters, observe that the felt bodily stances alluded to in the examples we have provided are typically connected to primitive scenarios, in which the emotion is felt in the presence of its object (de Sousa 1987: 181ff, Wollheim 1999). We are afraid of the dog because of the clear and present danger it poses, or ashamed because our privacy is exposed to the gaze of others. But of course the cognitive base of an emotion need not be a perception, and the emotion may be about something that is quite distant from these primitive scenarios. Situations eliciting fear or shame might go far beyond, respectively, those in which one's physical integrity is directly at stake or those that involve invasion of privacy and the reproving gaze of another. For instance, the disappearance of one's doctoral thesis from one's computer may elicit terror because of what it may imply for one's life prospects. Even if physical integrity is not directly at stake, one continues to feel the looming threat through the distinctive bodily attitude that is fear, though the actions undertaken will now be modulated by the specific context. Or consider anger. It may be the case that the sorts of primitive scenarios eliciting this emotion have to do with attempts to respond to a physical assault. But it is now, say, felt upon hearing of the abuse suffered by a child, and continues in this case to be experienced through the same distinctive bodily attitude. In this last case, note that, through recognition of the broader social implications of this type of situation, the emotional attitude involved has received another name, i.e. indignation. Now, whether or not the emotion gets relabeled, we face a phenomenon that we discussed in the foregoing (see Chapter 2, pp. 24–25), namely the fact that emotions, through the mediation of complex cognitive states, do get progressively calibrated to various types of situations because they share the relevant evaluative property with the primitive scenario, and for that reason make an emotional engagement of the kind involved in that scenario appropriate.

This now puts us in a position to explain how emotions get individuated on the present proposal. An emotion type is a type of felt bodily attitude towards objects that is correct if and only if these objects exemplify a given evaluative property. And thus, as in the theories of James and Prinz, there are as many emotions as there are structured wholes of bodily sensations, or, in the terms of our account, as many as there are distinctive felt bodily attitudes of the relevant type. As observed in Chapters 2 and 6, there are good reasons to think that there is a substantial number of these, and that we can understand the further distinctions drawn by ordinary languages as due to the fact that a subset of calibrated emotions is significant enough to receive a distinct label.[3] The present account thus satisfies a basic constraint on emotion theory: it has the resources to explain the variety of emotion types.

Other virtues of our version of the attitudinal theory emerge if we think of further important issues we discussed in connection with other approaches to the emotions. First, what is the direction of fit of emotional attitudes? Perhaps contrary to appearances, the fact that we have elucidated the nature of these attitudes in terms of felt action readiness does not mean that the emotions have the direction of fit characteristic of desires, i.e. aim at being satisfied or fulfilled (see Chapter 1, pp. 9–11). In emotion, one feels one's body poised to act in certain ways towards objects, say a perceived object. We have explained the sense in which these attitudes have correctness conditions, i.e. they are correct if the object exemplifies the relevant evaluative property and thus have the mind-to-world direction of fit. It is moreover plain that they do not have satisfaction or fulfillment conditions. There is no sense in which feeling one's body poised to act towards a perceived object, i.e. the emotional attitude, aims at being fulfilled. And observe that, if, in addition to aiming at fulfillment, desires, in virtue of being the attitudes they are, are correct if and only if the states of affairs they are about ought to obtain (see also Chapter 9, pp. 110–112), this is not the case for emotions. The latter are not correct or incorrect as a function of whether or not a state of affairs ought to obtain, but rather as a function of whether or not their object possesses the relevant evaluative property. These considerations constitute, we contend, decisive reasons for thinking that desires are not emotions.

That being said, we should hasten to add that emotions, because they are evaluative stances or attitudes we take towards the world, play a fundamental role in motivating subjects to act in specific ways and to form specific desires. Fear is an evaluative attitude, an attitude in the light of which the subject will typically form specific desires such as the desire to scamper up the nearest tree. Anger is an attitude in the light of which the subject will form the desire to avenge himself in this or that way. That is to say, the present approach to the emotions offers a neat solution to a fundamental problem facing the mixed theory of the emotions discussed in Chapter 3, namely the fact that some of the desires it appeals to in analyzing the emotions are more plausibly understood as desires motivated by these emotions than as constituent parts of them. Moreover, and for the same reasons, the attitudinal theory illuminates many of the relations between emotions and evaluative judgments, among other things why an evaluative judgment is often thought to imply that the judging subject is motivated to act accordingly. As we shall see in more detail in Chapter 10, it is because emotions provide the canonical conditions of application (Peacocke 1996) for the evaluative concepts we deploy in our evaluative judgments that these judgments connect so closely with motivation. The idea is that the circumstances (think of the primitive scenarios or more sophisticated elaborations of them) that elicit our emotional responses (i.e. the aforementioned distinct profiles of felt action readiness) constitute central and privileged conditions around which our mastery of the relevant evaluative concepts is built. These circumstances can have this function because the emotions they elicit are attitudes that are correct or incorrect depending on whether the relevant evaluative property is exemplified.

Now, this allows us to explain the intuition of many philosophers, according to whom the hallmark of a sincere evaluative judgment is being in the corresponding motivating state. Indeed, given that emotions provide us with canonical conditions of application for evaluative concepts, making an ordinary evaluative judgment involves saying, or at least implying, that a given emotional attitude is appropriate to the relevant situation, and that it would be suitable to be motivated in the way typical of the relevant emotion (e.g., Zagzebski 2004). In drawing such a distinction between emotions and evaluative judgments, the present approach, as a result, has a clear advantage over the evaluative judgment theory. The latter theory must, as we saw in Chapter 5, commit itself to a controversial form of motivational internalism about evaluative judgments in order to respect the intimate connection between emotion and motivation. The present approach explains the intuitions behind motivational internalism, without endorsing it, by emphasizing the fundamental role of emotional responses in shaping the evaluative concepts we deploy in making evaluative judgments.

Whatever the ramifications of this last observation for the problem of motivation (see e.g., Smith 1994), what is important to notice here is how the respective attitudes and contents of emotions, on the one hand, and of the corresponding judgments, on the other, differ insofar as the evaluative property is concerned. As we have seen, evaluative properties are not what the emotions are about; these properties generally do not figure in the content of the emotions. Rather, it is in virtue of being the very attitudes they are that the emotions come to have evaluative conditions of correctness. This contrasts with evaluative judgments where the evaluative correctness conditions trace back to the content. In making an evaluative judgment, we have the attitude of judging – the same attitude we have when we judge that an object is red, say – towards an object or situation of which we assert that it has a given evaluative property and for that reason perhaps imply that it makes a given emotional attitude appropriate. Undergoing the emotion, however, is precisely to exemplify the attitude which the corresponding evaluative judgment implies is appropriate to the object. As we shall see, the way in which the attitudinal theory articulates the links between emotions, desires, and evaluative judgments, respectively, will prove important in discussing some central epistemological questions surrounding the emotions in Chapters 8 to 10.

For now, note that, in clearly distinguishing emotions from evaluative judgments, the present account is well positioned to address some of the issues that sank the mixed theory (see Chapter 3) and the evaluative judgment theory (see Chapter 5) and turned theorists towards the perceptual approach. These issues, you will recall, are all connected with the fact that emotions should be conceived in such a way that we do not end up making unreasonable cognitive demands on the creatures that have them. And we must conceive of emotions in this way while explaining how emotions might form the basis upon which some concepts are learned and deployed. According to the attitudinal theory, animals and young infants can perfectly well have emotions without mastering the relevant evaluative concepts. To have an emotion it is enough to exemplify a felt bodily attitude of the right kind, and there are all the reasons in the world to think that animals and infants can do this. What they do not have, however, is the capacity to build on their emotional responses so as to come to understand that only some situations make them appropriate, that is, to make evaluative judgments. This in turn provides the resources to treat the cases of irrational emotions and phobias (see Chapter 5, pp. 54–55, and Chapter 6, p. 67). It is not difficult to see how one would come to adopt, on occasion or chronically, a given emotional attitude towards a certain situation while aware that the situation in question does not make it appropriate. And note in passing that the present account does not encourage an understanding of emotional errors or phobias on the model illustrated by perceptual illusions, as the perceptual theory does. In particular, within our account, phobias might well be fully irrational in the sense of being unjustified (see Chapter 8) and not merely mistaken, something that appears difficult to maintain if we think of them as akin to, say, optical illusions of the Müller-Lyer type. This concludes our examination of some key virtues of the attitudinal theory.

## Intentionality and phenomenology

It is important to assess now more generally the manner in which the present account fares with respect to the constraints that emerged from our discussion of the perceptual model of the emotions in Chapter 6. Remember: first, emotions stand in intentional relations to values without being about values (*intentionality constraint*). Second, emotions are essentially phenomenological states and stand in relation to values in virtue of being the phenomenological states they are (*phenomenology constraint*). Third, emotions are crucial, perhaps ineliminable, sources of justification for our evaluative judgments, even though they essentially depend on other cognitive states providing them with their objects (*epistemological constraint*). In the remainder of the chapter, we shall consider the two first constraints. The third constraint will be one of the central foci in the three last chapters of this book.

Regarding the *intentionality constraint*, the proposal holds that emotions indeed stand in intentional relations to evaluative properties, but that these intentional relations do not assume the form of emotions that have evaluative properties as their objects. Rather, as we have already stressed, the claim is that emotions are attitudes that are about the actual or potential bearers of evaluative properties, objects that we are aware of via other mental states – what we have called the cognitive bases of the emotions. Emotions are not experiences of these evaluative properties themselves but rather specific attitudes we adopt towards actual or potential bearers of evaluative properties, attitudes that are correct or incorrect depending on whether the object actually exemplifies the relevant evaluative property. And this is more than just a logical nicety of the present proposal.

Compare the attitudinal theory with the two perceptual models we previously outlined. In our opinion, any theory claiming that we *directly* perceive evaluative properties faces an intractable problem as soon as one realizes that most emotions have states other than perceptions as their cognitive bases. For what could it mean to say that we directly perceive the danger or offensiveness of a situation of which we are now presently aware only through imagination or thought? Regarding the emotions as attitudes we adopt towards objects, as opposed to direct perceptions of some of their properties, now removes the mystery surrounding the idea that we could have direct perceptual access to a subset of an object's properties (its evaluative properties), while the rest of them are, and can only be, accessed by other means, i.e. imagination or thought. The indirect model of how we perceive evaluative properties does not fare any better in this connection. We dismissed the manner in which James's model captures the intentionality of emotions because, as you will recall, the body ends up being the intentional object of the emotions. This problem does not go away even if, as Prinz argues, we could be in *indirect* contact with evaluative properties by being directly aware of bodily changes. For what lies at the root of this problem is the fact that there is intuitively no sense in which emotions are necessarily about the body (there are of course cases in which the content of the emotion, for one reason or another, makes reference to one's body). These worries do not arise within the attitudinal theory, for it does not conceive of emotions as being either about the body or about evaluative properties: the attitudinal theory, like that of Prinz, recruits profiles of bodily feelings, but it does it in a way that precludes any competition between the body and evaluative properties as candidate objects represented by emotions (see Chapter 6, pp. 72–73).

Now, the sense in which the attitudinal theory goes beyond the Jamesian picture just alluded to is best explained by considering the *phenomenological constraint*. Remember, the point here is not simply that there is something it is like to undergo an emotion, but that this experiential aspect of the emotions explains how they relate to evaluative properties. Most of the appeal of the perceptual model lies in the following analogy. In the same way as the phenomenology of perceptual experiences plays an essential role in making perceptual properties manifest to the subject, the phenomenology of emotional experiences plays an essential role in making evaluative properties manifest to the subject (e.g., Goldie 2009). And the cogency of this intuition appears to lie in the fact that we cannot conceive of the connection between, for instance, the phenomenology of fear and danger as arbitrary. Intuitively, no other emotional experience than that of fear is a suitable candidate for presenting the world in terms of a danger. Although we have no problem in understanding the fact that we might end up reacting to a dangerous situation with amusement, say, it is not intelligible to say that amusement makes the danger in the situation manifest to us. This intuition, which we accept, is at the root of the dissatisfaction we expressed regarding the neo-Jamesian approach (Chapter 6, pp. 72–73): the connection between the emotional experience and the evaluative property cannot be modeled on that between smoke and fire, namely as one of natural co-variation. Experiencing the evaluative property of an object is not taking the way one's body feels as an indication, a sign, or a symptom of the fact that this object has this property.

This difficulty is inescapable if one holds that the bodily experience of emotions takes an atomistic form: that of perceiving disturbances in specific bodily parts (one's heartbeat rising, contraction of the stomach, etc.). This may well be the right phenomenological description of what happens when we are no longer in the grip of the emotion but become aware of the trail it leaves in our body. For instance, this is what happens when you have just avoided a terrible road accident and you then contemplate the state of your body on the side of the road: you are acutely aware of a constellation of variously located bodily changes. But it seems incorrect as a phenomenological description of the role of the felt body in emotion, i.e. that of making salient aspects of the situation manifest. For you did not feel your body in this way when you were in the grip of fear at the sight of the truck barreling down towards you. The attitudinal theory avoids these problems by making a substantial phenomenological claim: in emotion, we feel a bodily attitude towards a given object, which amounts to saying that we feel the way our body is geared towards the object we are facing. The body is felt in the form of a gestalt of bodily sensations, which consists in being ready to respond in a given way to the object. If experiencing such an attitude is all there is to experiencing something in evaluative terms, then of course the relation between the attitude and the fact that the evaluative property enters into the correctness conditions of the mental state is anything but contingent. For the existence of such a relation between distinct emotions and distinct evaluative properties is not elucidated merely in terms of the existence of naturally selected patterns of co-variation between them, but rather in terms of the nature of the relevant attitudes themselves. And this, we believe, shows that the phenomenology constraint can be met without subscribing to a perceptual theory of the emotions.

We cannot close this discussion of the phenomenology of emotions without once again touching on the issues of transparency and valence that emerged in our discussion of the disanalogies between emotions and perceptions (see Chapter 6, pp. 68–69). If the attitudinal theory pictures the relation between the phenomenology of emotions and the evaluative property as anything but contingent, there is no requirement that the attitude represents the evaluative property transparently. Transparency, you will recall, is a property of the content of perceptual experiences and not one that is supposed to be possessed by any sort of attitude. That being the case, there is no requirement here that all the phenomenological aspects of the emotions, which will encompass echoes from the activation of various processes within the peripheral system, contribute to making it the evaluative attitude that it is. This, however, is what would have been required were emotions subject to transparency and what indeed seems required on the perceptual model.

Valence is another interesting aspect of emotional experiences. You will recall that this term of art refers to the fact that, unlike perceptual states, emotions are commonly classified as positive or negative (Chapter 2). While it may look as if the attitudinal theory leads naturally to a behavioral account of valence, it is in fact not tailored to fit any specific approach to the phenomenon. So let us briefly review the different approaches to valence from the perspective of the attitudinal theory. Although it is for the most part – but not always – possible to classify felt bodily stances as tendencies to approach or to withdraw, note that the verdict we come to by applying this distinction often does not correspond to our intuitions as to which emotions are positive or negative. Loving affection and anger are both inclinations to approach, but we tend to think of the former as positive and the latter as negative. This is because the abstract properties of being inclinations to approach or to withdraw paper over the richness and fine nuances characteristic of the different emotions understood as profiles of felt action readiness. For example, the account does not capture the fact that some of these profiles are pleasant, others unpleasant. When this is the case, it surely makes sense to call an emotion positive or negative in the sense favored by the hedonic tone approach to valence. Still, there is no reason to presume that this will cover all cases, as some of these profiles are neither pleasant nor unpleasant (think of anger). We must reach exactly the same verdict as regards the idea that positive and negative emotions correspond to (representations of) satisfied and frustrated desires. Not all emotions, as we have seen in Chapter 3, align with the fortune of our desires – we tend for instance to think of admiration as a positive emotion, yet admiration need not presuppose the relevant desires. As to the idea that positive emotions are those one desires to continue experiencing, negative emotions those one desires to cease to experience, the following should be observed. First, it is far from clear that the relevant desires systematically accompany our emotional attitudes. Second, when they do accompany them, they are motivated by these attitudes and are not constitutive parts of them. It is indeed not uncommon for joy to motivate a desire that it persists.

There is then no shortage of competing criteria seeking to account for the valence of emotions. In addition to those featuring in these contemporary approaches, we may think of criteria pertaining to the (in)appropriateness of the emotions or to their moral and prudential (dis)value, and perhaps also criteria resulting from the various reasons one might have to carve the evaluative domain into positive and negative values. What this brief survey seems to suggest, then, is that while the attitudinal theory accommodates the various intuitions underlying different approaches to valence, it does not foster any one in particular. This is a consequence we believe should be welcomed. Given the variety of reasons for which attitudes may be classified as positive or negative, the often-voiced skepticism regarding the unity of the phenomenon (e.g., Solomon 2003) is far from unwarranted. This liberal approach to valence concludes our discussion of the way the attitudinal theory satisfies the phenomenology constraint.

# Conclusion

We suggested that emotions are fruitfully approached through the contrast between attitude and content. More specifically, we argued that distinct emotions are distinct attitudes that we take towards the objects provided by their cognitive bases.[4] This allows us to understand the connection between emotions and evaluative properties in terms of the way distinct attitudes contribute to emotions' correctness conditions. Elaborating on the idea of emotions as attitudes in light of the journey completed until this point, we then defended the following idea: each emotion consists in a specific felt bodily stance towards objects or situations, which is correct or incorrect as a function of whether or not these objects and situations exemplify the relevant evaluative property. We then argued that this approach to the emotions compares favorably with perceptual theories as regards the intentionality and phenomenology of the emotions.

# Questions and further readings

(1)   What are the advantages of locating the connection between emotions and evaluative properties at the level of the attitude rather than at the level of the content?

(2)   How should emotional attitudes be conceived so as to account for the fact that they are evaluative attitudes?

(3)   Which account of valence, if any, is fostered by the attitudinal theory?

While the distinction between *attitude* or *mode* on the one hand and *content* on the other is extensively used, there is not much in the literature about the nature of this distinction. Searle (1983) still constitutes a very good starting point, while Crane (1998, 2007) provides careful and illuminating discussions. Mulligan (2004) is an important reference regarding the connections between attitudes and formal objects. For an application of the idea that the various attitudes or modes should not be elucidated at the level of their content, with a special emphasis on perception and memory, see Récanati (2007).

Dewey (1895) and Binet (1910) are early attempts at understanding James's bodily feelings in terms of (felt) bodily attitudes. Claparède does the same in his outstanding article (1928) in which he puts forwards his account of the emotions as *evaluative attitudes* and comes very close to our own theory. Bull's (1951/1968) 'attitude theory of the emotions' is a cogent empirically grounded defense of the idea that emotions are feelings of preparedness. Frijda (1986, 2007) has done more than anybody else to stress the fundamental role of action readiness and to provide rich phenomenological descriptions of the phenomena. Lambie and Marcel (2002), Colombetti (2007), as well as the Heidegger-inspired Slaby (2008) and Ratcliffe (2008), provide numerous cues for enriching these descriptions.

## Notes

1 We use the term 'attitudes' where others use the terms 'modes' or 'intentional modes'. Using this term has the slight disadvantage of suggesting that the relevant phenomena must be directed at propositions – an implication we most certainly do not want, as we shall shortly see – but has, as our account will make clear, the advantage of reflecting the manner in which emotions are directed towards their contents quite nicely.

2 It is interesting to note that Solomon (2002), in his later works and under pressure to explain how his theory of the emotions in terms of evaluative judgments can accommodate the fact that emotions are essentially felt, seems to refer precisely to this idea when, also quoting Frijda, he speaks of the 'kinesthetic judgments' involved in the emotions.

3 But see Chapter 2, Note 1.

4 An interesting issue raised by the account offered here concerns the relations between the nature of the mental state that functions as the cognitive basis of the emotion and the emotional attitude itself. In this chapter, we have conducted our discussion as if emotions always had 'serious' or 'assertive' mental states such as perceptions and beliefs as their bases. But of course we also have emotions, or perhaps quasi-emotions (Walton 1990), based on 'non serious' or 'non assertive' mental states such as episodes of imagination. One question concerns whether and how emotional attitudes can reflect the fact that they are based on such 'non assertive' states, a question that is of central interest for elucidating the nature of our emotional involvement with fiction.

# 8    Emotions and their justification

In Chapter 6, we saw that one central motivation for perceptual theories of the emotions is the claim that the epistemological relation between emotions and evaluative judgments mirrors that between perceptions and perceptual judgments: in both cases, the experience typically causes and potentially justifies the judgment. Now, the fact that we often make evaluative judgments as a causal result of the emotions we experience (e.g., Mary judges the remark to be offensive because she is angry at its author) is something that we have already emphasized. Whether emotions can in addition justify evaluative judgments is an important question that we shall address in due course (see Chapter 10), but not before the question as to the conditions under which the emotions themselves are justified is answered. Recall that this last question is one that can hardly be asked from within the framework of perceptual theories since, modeling emotions on perceptions as they do, they fail to recognize that emotions are states for which we ask for reasons. Yet it is not unusual to ask why we have the emotions we have.

For this and further reasons, we defended in the previous chapter the claim that emotions are attitudes that we adopt towards contents provided by other mental states that we called their cognitive bases. More specifically, we have said that distinct emotional attitudes are correct when the object provided by their cognitive bases exemplifies the relevant evaluative property. Emphasizing in this way the role of cognitive bases puts us in an ideal position to investigate epistemological issues that were masked from the perspective of perceptual theories. In the present chapter, we investigate the conditions that must be satisfied by these cognitive bases in order for emotional attitudes based on them to be justified. In this way, the first part of the epistemological constraint that we said any satisfactory theory of the emotions should satisfy will be met: emotions will be pictured as epistemologically dependent on their bases. After examining in Chapter 9 the epistemological consequences of the fact that a subject's motivational set is also an important determinant of the emotions he experiences, we shall finally be in a position, in Chapter 10, to meet the second part of our epistemological constraint: we shall explain in what sense emotions play important epistemological roles vis-à-vis the evaluative judgments they typically trigger in spite of their own epistemological dependence on cognitive bases.

In this chapter, we shall first show the need for an account of justified emotions by elaborating on the central disanalogy between the respective epistemological roles of emotions and perceptions vis-à-vis the judgments they explain. In a nutshell, the possibility of asking why-questions about the emotions shows that they are, unlike perceptions, states for which we have or lack reasons. Next, we reject an epistemological picture – one according to which emotions are preceded by evaluative judgments or value intuitions – a picture that this disanalogy may encourage but that we regard as unconvincing. On the basis of this conclusion, we then develop an account of justified emotions. We observe that why-questions about the emotions can be answered by reference to the emotions' cognitive and motivational bases. We then focus on cognitive bases, and put forward the claim that an emotion is justified if, and only if, the properties the subject is (or seems to be) aware of (would) constitute an instance of the evaluative property that features in the correctness conditions of this emotion. Finally, we answer various objections according to which this analysis is insufficient.

## Why-questions: perceptions vs. emotions

Let us return to the epistemological picture fostered by perceptual theories of the emotions, which attempt to model the epistemology of evaluative judgments on that of perceptual judgments, by examining the conditions under which perceptual judgments are justified. It is reasonable to think that you are justified in judging that there is a red circle in front of you when you have an experience as of a red circle, and no reason to consider this experience illusory or otherwise misleading. That is to say, perceptual experiences provide defeasible justification for perceptual judgments (e.g., Pollock 1974: Chapter 5).[1] Straightforwardly modeling the epistemology of evaluative judgments on that of perceptual judgments would then suggest that an emotion defeasibly justifies the corresponding evaluative judgment in the absence of reasons to think it is incorrect. Say you are amused by a joke or afraid of a dog and have no reason to think that your emotional response is incorrect. It may then appear reasonable to think that your judgments – that the joke is funny and the dog dangerous – are defeasibly justified.

Now, notwithstanding the reasons for which epistemologists maintain that perceptual experiences justify perceptual judgments – because these experiences put us in direct cognitive contact with the relevant objects and properties, because these experiences are reliably caused by them, etc. – the basic appeal of this claim can be traced back to the following: answers to *why-questions* concerning perceptual judgments reach rock bottom when reference is made to a perceptual experience that there is no reason to distrust. 'I (seem to) see one' is a good and – other things being equal – ultimate answer to 'Why do you think there is a yellow station wagon in the street?' The way we conceive of perceptual experiences as apt to end the quest for justification in this way is surely symptomatic of our conceiving of them as primary modes of access to the relevant objects and properties.

None of these points apply to the emotions, however. Not only do emotions provide odd answers to the relevant *why-questions*, but even when we accept them as such they clearly do not end the quest for justification in relation to evaluative judgments. Thus, even if 'I am angry about it' can provide an answer to the question 'Why do you think the remark is offensive?', we are likely to go on and ask 'But why are you angry about it?' and expect the answer to provide more than a mere causal explanation.

This observation makes it obvious that emotions are states for which we have or lack reasons, i.e. states that, in stark contrast to perceptual experiences, can be justified or not. Now, the fact that emotions are states for which we have or lack reasons suggests that they are not primary modes of access to evaluative properties in the way visual perception is a primary mode of access to the sizes, shapes, and colors of objects in our immediate vicinity. The possibility of asking the further question 'But why are you angry?' seems rather to suggest that emotions should be conceived of as reactions to the subject's *prior* and *non-emotional* awareness of evaluative properties ('Well, the remark is obviously very offensive!'). Should we go along with this suggestion and claim, as does Brady for example, that emotions are preceded by 'non-emotional abilities to recognize and identify' (2010: 126) evaluative properties in order to explain the striking epistemological disanalogy between emotions and perceptions? This is indeed an option, but we still need to be clear about what these abilities precisely amount to. And in fact, as we shall now argue, as soon as we try to cash out what these abilities may consist in, the plausibility of the option becomes questionable.

## Value judgments and value intuitions

If the reasons we typically offer in defense of emotions refer to the object's evaluative properties, we may want to explain this fact by suggesting that the relevant abilities are deployed in the making of evaluative judgments: one possibility, then, is that justified emotions are reactions to justified evaluative judgments. The claim is that one experiences justified fear of the dog only if one has come to a justified judgment as to its dangerousness, as one experiences justified shame only after having justifiably judged that one's action is degrading. Now we have already commented on the shortcomings of theories according to which emotions are or presuppose evaluative judgments (see Chapter 5). Still, while they may have failed as accounts of the emotions, they might still be correct as accounts of *justified* emotions.

Granted, but note first how unconvincing this conception of justified emotions is. It just does not seem right to count as unjustified all those emotions that are obviously not preceded by endorsements of the relevant propositional contents. We do not question the justification of a person's anger upon, say, being verbally abused for his origins simply because his anger is not based on a judgment about the offensiveness of the remark. Second, this picture puts a strange spin on the problem as we set it up at the beginning of this chapter. We took it for granted that evaluative judgments are often made as a result of the emotions we undergo. But if we go along with the conception under discussion, and claim that justified emotions depend on evaluative judgments, then we simply cannot use the former to explain (and potentially justify) the latter.[2] Third and relatedly, this conception is unable to resolve the problem raised by the existence of why-questions about the emotions. Evaluative judgments are not legitimate end-stations in the quest for justifying emotions, since they themselves stand in need of justification; why we make these evaluative judgments is after all the question we started with.

If the subject's awareness of the reasons for his emotions does not take the form of an evaluative judgment, then an attractive alternative would consist in regarding the relevant 'non-emotional ability to identify' evaluative properties as an intellectually less demanding type of evaluative cognition: emotions are reactions to value intuitions or, as Mulligan suggests (2007, 2010), to apparent or real feelings of value. One's fear of the dog is justified if and only if it is a reaction to one's intuiting (or seeming to intuit) its dangerousness. However, while this suggestion does not fall prey to the same problems as the claim that emotions depend on evaluative judgments, it faces some serious difficulties of its own.

First, the claim that we are endowed with a capacity to intuit evaluative properties reminds us of an idea we treated in connection with Goldie's idea that emotions are, or contain, feelings towards (see Chapter 6, p. 70). Talk of value intuitions similarly suggests a sort of immediate, quasi-perceptual acquaintance with evaluative properties. Yet, as we have seen, no convincing evidence in favor of the existence of such a form of acquaintance has been adduced, and we are as a result left in the dark about its nature. Second and relatedly, if value intuitions are regarded as a distinct *sui generis* type of mental state, then they just look like *ad hoc* postulates introduced so as to resolve the present epistemological problem. Not only have we been presented with no positive reason to think that value intuitions exist, but we shall see below that the problem they are introduced to solve can be resolved without appealing to them.[3] Third, the claim that value intuitions can solve the epistemological problem raised by the existence of why-questions about the emotions is also open to discussion. Is it plausible to maintain that an emotion is justified simply because it is grounded in such an intuition? If the only thing you have to say in favor of your anger is that you somehow intuited the offensiveness of a remark that strikes others as perfectly innocent, then you will no doubt fail to alter their assessment of your anger as unjustified.

So, not only do the two conceptions we have discussed here face serious difficulties, they also fail to solve the problem we are trying to address. And they fail to solve it for the same reason: the alleged non-emotional ability to identify evaluative properties cannot take the form of evaluative judgments or value intuitions, since neither put an end to the justification regress. We should therefore reject the idea that justified emotions depend on evaluative judgments or value intuitions. If that is so, then what if anything puts an end to the justification of emotions? The answer requires taking a closer look at why-questions about the emotions, a task to which we now turn.

## Back to why-questions

In order to build an alternative account of justified emotions, we should be careful to distinguish two kinds of answers to why-questions about the emotions.

First, why-questions are typically answered by reference to the various *cognitive bases* that emotions may have. As we have often observed, the occurrence of an emotion, unlike the occurrence of a perception, always presupposes a mental state that is about the object of the emotion. Perception provides a direct access to objects and facts in the sense that it does not depend on another mental state directed at these very objects and facts. Emotions must, by contrast, latch on to objects provided by (virtually any) other types of mental state, such as perceptions, of course, but also memories, or beliefs.

Answers to why-questions of the first kind refer to the content of these cognitive bases or some salient feature thereof. 'Why are you afraid of the lion?'; 'Well, I see it staring at me and approaching fast!' The answer proceeds here by explaining the subject's *way of apprehending* those aspects of the situation in light of which her emotional attitude is assessed as correct or incorrect. Often the question will be due to the questioner's ignorance of some features of that situation, and it is sensibly answered by reference to the content of the subject's cognitive base. Full answers along these lines proceed by mentioning some further properties of the subject as well as some relations between her and the emotion's object. In the lion case, such an answer would mention, say, the facts that the subject is made of flesh and blood as well as some spatial and other relations between her and the animal.

Of course, the issue is more complicated when emotions are based on mental states like beliefs that can be assessed, in turn, as justified or not. You may for instance know that Sylvia owns a lot of German bonds and know that their value will be substantially affected if BMW is sold to a Chinese corporation, yet question the justification of her fear by querying her belief that BMW is going to be sold. 'Why is she afraid she will lose her fortune?' should in this context be understood as 'Why does she think she might lose her fortune?' And here, you may be satisfied on learning that Sylvia has access to insider information according to which the deal is very likely. Simple or more complex answers to why-questions proceeding along these lines we call *cognitive base* answers.

Second, why-questions can receive another kind of answer because the occurrence of emotions is often, if not always, susceptible to rich explanations in terms of the subject's motivational set. In this, once again, emotions contrast in some important respects with perceptual states. Moods, temperaments, character traits, and sentiments often prove crucial for the occurrence of an emotion. An episode of shame may for instance be explained by one's prudishness (character trait), and we understand Mark's pride at a little girl winning a prize when we learn that she is his beloved niece (sentiment). Answers to why questions that proceed along these lines we shall call, for lack of a better term, *motivational base* answers.

What exactly these affective states and dispositions are shall be explored in the next chapter, when we investigate their impact on the epistemology of emotions. For the rest of the present chapter, we shall focus on the epistemological role of the emotions' cognitive bases. The crucial point at this stage is to observe that cognitive base answers to why-questions do not typically seem to refer to value judgments or value intuitions. Does this mean that we can develop an account of justified emotions that dispenses with them?

## Justified emotions

The cognitive base of an emotion then need not, and typically does not, contain an evaluative judgment or a value intuition. This is for instance the case when fear is explained by the subject's awareness of a dog with big teeth behaving erratically. If we think for that reason emotions can be justified independently of antecedent evaluative judgments or value intuitions, there must of course be an intimate relation between the content of the cognitive base and the emotion that this cognitive base explains, a relation that makes room for the claim that awareness of the former justifies the latter. And, since emotional attitudes have correctness conditions that must be couched in evaluative terms, this means that awareness of the cognitive base's content must be able to justify a mental state that is correct if, and only if, a given evaluative property is exemplified. So, what relation must hold between the content of the cognitive base and the evaluative property featuring in the emotion's correctness conditions, such that awareness of the content of the cognitive base justifies the emotion?

At this juncture, we have to briefly return to what we said in the conclusion of our discussion of the metaphysical links between emotions and evaluative properties (Chapter 4, pp. 49–50). Commenting on the shortcomings of various attempts at analyzing the nature of evaluative properties in terms of emotional responses, we said that evaluative properties supervene on natural properties. The relation we are now after is, we suggest, one of strong supervenience between evaluative and non-evaluative properties. To say that an evaluative property strongly supervenes on a non-evaluative property (or a set of such properties) is a way of saying that whenever an object exemplifies the former it does so in virtue of or because it exemplifies the latter: we face a relation of constitution holding between one type of property and another (e.g., Dancy 1993: Chapter 5). Without entering into details, the important idea for our present purposes is simply that an object exemplifies a given evaluative property at a given time, and in a given context, in virtue of exemplifying some non-evaluative properties. For instance, at a given time and in a given context, a dog's dangerousness is constituted by its having big teeth and its behaving unpredictably.[4]

This creates an opening for an alternative account of justified emotions, since it allows for the possibility that the properties on which an evaluative property supervenes feature in the content of mental states that are neither evaluative judgments nor value intuitions. There is for instance no need to judge that the dog is dangerous or to somehow intuit its dangerousness in order to be aware of its big teeth and unpredictable behavior. And this suggests the following account of justified emotions:

> An emotion is justified if, and only if, in the situation in which the subject finds herself, the properties she is (or seems to be) aware of and on which her emotion is based constitute (or would constitute) an exemplification of the evaluative property that features in the correctness conditions of the emotion she undergoes.

Suppose that a dog with big teeth that is behaving in an impulsive way constitutes, given the circumstances in which the subject finds herself, a danger. The idea is that her fear is justified if it is based on her awareness of this dog, its big teeth and impulsive behavior. The epistemological claim distinctive of this account is thus that, if a relation of constitution obtains, awareness of the properties that constitute the evaluative property justifies an emotion whose correctness conditions make reference to that property. Consequently, justified emotions need not be based on evaluative judgments or value intuitions.

Still, the idea that justified fear must ultimately rest on an apprehension in evaluative terms of that which makes the fear correct, and that this apprehension must take the form of an evaluative judgment or a value intuition, may seem obvious. Yet this idea should cease to be obvious once the subject is credited with an awareness of properties that constitute danger (Jackson 1998: 127). For, if danger is constituted by the instantiation of some non-evaluative properties, there is no further fact of the matter, nothing more to a specific danger than the instantiation of what makes it a danger. In a given context, a dog with big teeth and impulsive behavior constitutes a danger, as the death of a person may constitute a loss, or a specific remark may constitute an offense. A specific instance of danger, loss, or offensiveness is not a further property alongside those properties that constitute it (Dancy 1993: 75). If awareness of these properties explains why a subject undergoes the relevant emotion, then this emotion is explained by the subject's awareness of an instance of the relevant evaluative property. And this seems sufficient to justify it.

According to this account, then, the emotion's justification depends on the subject being aware, through its cognitive base, of a content apt to justify it. Now, crediting the subject with such awareness is unproblematic in many cases, as when the emotion is based on perceptions or memories, for we paradigmatically have access to these states and their contents. Things may seem different, however, when the cognitive base is constituted by a belief whose justification depends, say, on the validity of a complex inference. For Sylvia's fear to be justified, what sort of access should she have to the complex reasons that support her belief that she might lose her fortune? The soundness of our account is, it seems to us, unaffected however the question is answered. We may think that the subject must be aware of the complete chain of reasons for her belief that she might lose her fortune. Or we may be satisfied with the requirement that they are readily available to her. More modestly yet, we may only require that she formed these beliefs at some point and has not changed her mind. While we incline towards the latter, an informed verdict on this count would lead to complex issues in epistemology that lie outside the purview of an introduction to the emotions. In any case, whatever option should ultimately be favored, it is in our opinion compatible with the account of justified emotions on offer. We shall now elaborate on this account by discussing the claim that it does not do justice to the nature of the emotions' cognitive bases.

## Bridging the gaps

This account is likely to raise the following serious worry. There seems to be *an important gap* between awareness of properties constituting an instance of an evaluative property and what justifies a given emotion. After all, it seems possible for a subject aware of these properties to fail to grasp their 'normative significance', that is, that they are the reasons they are. According to the present worry, this shows that, to justify an emotion, awareness of a specific danger must be supplemented by awareness of its normative significance, which consists in making an evaluative judgment.[5]

There are three distinct interpretations of the claim that one might fail to grasp the normative significance of a danger one is aware of: (a) the idea might be that being aware of a danger is not sufficient to *explain the occurrence* of fear; (b) it might be that this is not sufficient for one to realize that one faces a *motivationally relevant* situation; (c) finally, one might think that it is insufficient to explain one's realizing that danger is *apt to justify* one's emotion. The suggested upshot is that, whichever of these interpretations one favors, the existence of a gap shows that emotions in general or justified emotions more specifically require the making of evaluative judgments. So, let us consider these interpretations in turn.

(a) Note that, in the presentation of our account, we have only laid out a condition on the contents of cognitive bases that we think is sufficient to *justify* the emotions they explain, and we have said nothing about what is required for awareness of the former to *explain* the occurrence of the latter. Furthermore, it is correct to point out, in line with the first interpretation of what the gap consists in, that awareness of a content meeting this condition is not sufficient to explain why an emotion occurs. Awareness of a specific danger is for instance insufficient to explain the occurrence of fear: when discussing the typical answers to why-questions about the emotions, we have seen that one's motivational profile, including moods, temperaments, affective dispositions, character traits, and sentiments, is likely to play a crucial role in such explanations, and we shall investigate in the next chapter what this shows about the justification of emotions. For now, we want to focus on the following challenge. Is it not the case that combining the relevant motivational state with the awareness of an instance of a given evaluative property is still insufficient to explain why the emotion occurs? One can after all be aware of a specific danger, be motivated to preserve one's physical integrity, yet not feel afraid. Granted. But it is unclear how this challenge could concern an account of justified emotions. Such an account should not obviously be required to explain why some emotions do not occur. Yet, since the appeal to evaluative judgments in connection with the emotions is typically motivated by worries pertaining to why emotions occur, which may in turn lead to epistemological worries, we think this is the right place to address this issue. So, does this challenge show that we should supplement our account with evaluative judgments? Here is why we do not think so.

First, in many instances it is simply wrong to think that the possibility envisaged by the challenge can arise. In the most primitive cases, the subject is simply 'wired' in such a way that perceptual awareness of some properties elicits an emotion. This is in all probability the case in situations we have described in terms of an emotion's 'primitive scenario' (Chapter 7, p. 82), such as the fear predators elicit in some animals, and, more generally, those emotions we have understood as affect programs (Chapter 2, pp. 18–20).

Second, explaining why emotions are elicited in more complex cases need not refer to evaluative judgments. A subject may for instance have to learn that animals with such and such features are likely to attack. Through such learning, perception of the relevant properties gets associated with the likelihood of an attack and elicits fear. Yet, even though the subject's response clearly depends on her having gone through a certain learning process, it would be a complete misrepresentation of how this learning manifests itself to think that it has to involve the making of an evaluative judgment: we only need to credit her with a specific recognitional capacity.[6] Once she possesses this capacity, which partly explains why her emotion occurs, the justification of her fear depends on whether it is due to (real or merely apparent) perceptual awareness of properties constituting danger. Whether or not she had to learn to discriminate the relevant properties, these are cases in which the emotion is justified because it is based on a perception with a specific content.[7]

Now, as we have seen, the justification of emotions does of course not always take this form. When the emotion is based on a non-perceptual belief, there is room for further epistemological questions that target the justification of this belief. Is Sylvia's belief that she might lose her fortune, a belief on which her fear is based, justified? In these more complex cases, the subject cannot access the relevant properties through perception, but only via complex cognitive states. In order to feel fear, Sylvia must for instance have connected her concern with her own well-being with complex facts about the working of various financial institutions and how they are likely to affect the stock market and therefore her assets. And here it may be the case that mastery of the relevant evaluative concept is needed for her to extend in this way the range of situations likely to elicit her fear. But the fact that her present response depends on a learning process that is surely very complex does not support, any more than in the purely perceptual cases just discussed, the idea that her fear must be preceded by the making of an evaluative judgment. What we should rather say is that she is now, in virtue of this complex learning process, apt to directly react with fear to various situations.

Nonetheless, settling the question regarding the explanations of the occurrence of emotions in this way may be thought to create the following problem. Is it not the case that what happened during the learning process contributes now to the justification of the emotion? Should we not say, for instance, that Sylvia's past evaluative judgments contribute to the justification of the fear she presently feels? This problem is, we believe, more apparent than real. If these past evaluative judgments were justified, then they were justified by her justified beliefs regarding the direction the stock market was taking, etc. And this is exactly what we should say about her present fear: if it is justified, then it is in virtue of her justified beliefs about the direction the stock market is now taking, etc.

Now, of course, an account of justified emotions along these lines, which makes reference only to the content of the subject's cognitive base, is sufficient only if the subject's concerns (e.g., Sylvia's concern for her financial well-being) do not contribute to the justification of her emotions. We will offer reasons in favor of this last claim in Chapter 9.

(b) Let us now turn to the second interpretation of what the gap consists in, i.e. the claim that there is nothing in our account to ensure that the subject realizes that he faces a *motivationally relevant* situation. On this second interpretation, it is difficult to see why evaluative judgments would fare any better than emotions in bridging the gap. Indeed, while emotions are, according to most theories, and certainly ours, directly motivating states, no such thing is true of evaluative judgments unless contentious forms of motivational internalism are shown to be correct (see Chapter 5, p. 54 and Chapter 7, p. 84). Emotions, we have argued, are attitudes consisting in a readiness to act in various and distinctive ways vis-à-vis a given object or situation. That being so, if realizing that the situation one faces is normatively significant means grasping its motivational relevance, the fact that a subject undergoes an emotion based on the content of his awareness is enough to constitute in and of itself a grasp of its normative significance. That much is not true, or at least not obviously true, of a subject who only judges that the situation exemplifies a given evaluative property.

(c) Assessing the third interpretation of what the gap consists in is less straightforward. Its motivation is best understood in light of the family of views we referred to as fitting attitude analyses and criticized in Chapter 4, views according to which an object has a given evaluative property if and only if a given emotion towards it would be appropriate. Now, such a normative approach to evaluative properties may move one to raise the following worry: our account misses the fact that a justified emotion presupposes that the subject is aware or has the impression *that this emotion is (would be) appropriate*. Indeed, neither the subject's awareness of the situation (awareness, say, of a dog with sharp teeth), nor his having the emotion (fearing the dog) is identical to awareness that it is appropriate to be afraid: emotions cannot refer to their own appropriateness in that way (Brady 2010). It follows, or so the story goes, that we again have to appeal to evaluative judgments: having a justified emotion requires awareness that it is appropriate, and this awareness can only consist in the making of the judgment that it is the case.

This conception of justified emotions has little to recommend it, however. First, it flies in the face of the phenomenology. When we undergo emotions, we seem to be entirely directed 'outwards' to the world and its properties, and in no way 'inwards' to responses that would be appropriate in the circumstances (Tappolet 2011). Whether or not it is justified, an episode of sadness, anger, or amusement does not seem to be preceded by a mental act checking up on the normative credentials such emotions would possess. Second, this normative approach to evaluative judgments appears to require the existence of properties exemplified in the circumstances and able to justify the emotions that respond to them. As we insisted in our discussion of fitting attitude analyses, when the predicates 'appropriate' and 'justified' are applied to the emotions, they mean what they are customarily taken to mean in other areas of discourse, namely that there are good and undefeated reasons for representing the facts as these emotions do (see Chapter 4, pp. 48–49). Only in this way can we make sense of why the corresponding evaluative judgments deem them appropriate. It is by reference to evaluative properties that we explain why the relevant norms bear on the circumstances: one ought to be afraid because the situation is dangerous, one ought to admire this painting because it is beautiful. The strongest interpretation of what the gap in our account may consist in then yields no reason to give it up.

## Conclusion

In Chapter 7, we defended the idea that emotions are distinct attitudes that are correct when their objects, inherited from their cognitive bases, exemplify the relevant evaluative property. In this chapter, taking as our point of departure the differences between perceptions and emotions as regards the possibility of asking why-questions, we focused on the epistemological role of the emotions' cognitive bases. We argued that an emotion is justified if and only if the properties apprehended through the cognitive base for this emotion constitute or would constitute an instance of the evaluative property that features in its correctness conditions. Finally, we addressed an important group of worries linked to a potential gap between the conditions laid down by our account and justified emotions. We argued that, if the gap is understood along explanatory lines, then we should credit the subject with the relevant recognitional capacities. If we prefer to understand it along motivational lines, then we have suggested that emotions themselves can bridge it. And when understood along normative lines, we showed that it betrays a presupposition that the justification of emotions should be exclusively elucidated in the light of the fact that evaluative judgments normatively comment on them, a presupposition that revealed itself to be deeply flawed.

## Questions and further readings

(1)    We do not request reasons for perceptions in the way we do for emotions. Explain.

(2)    How is the proposed account of justified emotions informed by the idea that evaluative properties supervene on natural properties?

(3)    Are there reasons to think that the account of justified emotions on offer is insufficient?

The most helpful references for the relation of *constitution* at the core of our account of justified emotions are Dancy (1993: Chapter 5, 2004: 85ff), who describes it as a relation of *resultance*. Strandberg (2008) convincingly argues that the notions of constitution and resultance Dancy appeals to can be explained in terms of strong supervenience. For a very helpful introduction to the general issue, see Jackson (1998) and, for an extended but difficult treatment of the metaphysics of values centered on the problem of their relations to natural properties, see Oddie (2005).

For a very interesting and helpful introduction to *epistemology in connection to the emotions* (in French, however), see Tappolet (2000). The same book defends an account of the epistemological role of emotions modeled on that of perception, as do Deonna (2006), Döring (2007, 2009), and Elgin (1996, 2008). The most forceful critique of this approach from the perspective of the fitting attitude analysis can be found in Brady (2010, 2011). Dokic and Lemaire (2012) also stress the limits of the perceptual analogy in accounting for the epistemological role of emotions. Goldie's (2004b) excellent discussion comes closest to the account of justified emotions we advocate. A collection of essays covering some of the issues discussed in this chapter is Brun, Doğuoğlu, and Kuenzle (2008).

## Notes

1  We skip over complications raised in this connection by some disjunctivist positions claiming that only perceptions, as opposed to other perceptual experiences, like illusions and hallucinations, justify. As far as we can see, this does not affect our discussion.

2  Perhaps the most we could then say is that the absence of an emotion after having made the relevant evaluative judgment may sometimes defeat one's justification for making it ('why do I

think it is funny if I am not amused in the slightest?'). For an interesting discussion of this problem, see D'Arms and Jacobson (2010).

3 This criticism of course does not apply if by 'value intuitions' one means to refer to the emotions themselves. For such an approach, see Roeser (2011).

4 These formulations make it clear that we do not suggest that the supervenience base for evaluative properties only comprises monadic properties of the relevant object. The supervenience base will typically comprise relational properties of this object as well as some properties of the subject undergoing the emotion. It is crucial to keep this in mind for the remainder of our discussion.

5 It may also consist in intuiting a value. However, in the absence of a full-fledged account of what value intuitions are, it is unclear whether they possess the normative credentials that cognitive bases supposedly lack, and thus how the points to be developed here apply to them.

6 While there is an ongoing debate within psychology and neuroscience (see e.g., LeDoux 1996: Chapter 3) as to whether or not the exercise of these recognitional capacities takes the form of the making of implicit or unconscious evaluative judgments, there is ample reason to think that none of the subpersonal processes described in this debate will count as evaluative judgments or intuitions of value as these are portrayed in the philosophical debate that interests us here (see Pugmire 1998: Chapter 2). It is for very similar reasons that Prinz, when he introduces *calibration files* (2004: 99–102), i.e. structures in long-term memory that allow emotions to be elicited by variously complex external factors, explicitly denies that their activation amounts to the making of the relevant evaluative judgment.

7 The number of cases belonging to this class will vary as a function of the kinds of properties that can be accessed by purely perceptual means. For a discussion of this issue, see Siegel (2006).

# 9 The nature and role of affective explanations

In Chapter 8, we defended the idea that an emotion is justified if, and only if, the properties the subject is aware of thanks to the cognitive base of his emotion constitute an instance of the evaluative property that features in its correctness conditions. To develop this account, we focused exclusively on those answers to why-questions about the emotions that connect with their cognitive bases, that is, the perceptions, memories, beliefs, etc. that explain why the subject experiences a given emotion. We saw, however, that answers involving cognitive bases provide only part of the explanation of why emotions occur: what we have called motivational states should also be counted amongst the determinants of emotional responses. My disappointment at the ice-cream vendor's answer only makes sense given my desire to try the *fior di latte* flavor (desire), my anger at the store manager should be explained by my grumpiness (mood), my shame by the fact that I am attached to privacy (character trait), and my pride at this little girl winning the prize becomes clear upon learning that she is my beloved niece (sentiment).

This chapter has two main aims. The first is to describe these different motivational states and to understand their roles in explanations of the emotions. We shall argue that explaining emotions in terms of moods and temperaments is tantamount to providing arational explanations for their occurrence. For this reason, explanations that proceed in these terms serve to point to the *un*justified character of the emotion. Explanations of emotions in terms of character traits, sentiments, and desires are, by contrast, largely rational in the sense that they serve to locate an emotion within the subject's broader evaluative perspective. This is true even though appeal to these states also sometimes serves to question the justification of the emotions thereby explained. Our second aim will then consist in measuring more generally the epistemological impact, negative and positive, of these motivational states on the emotions. Regarding their negative impact, we shall offer reasons to think that even if motivational states sometimes have a distorting effect on our emotions, this is no reason to abandon the account we have defended in Chapter 8. Regarding their positive role, we shall present and offer reasons to reject two views according to which motivational states are justificatory reasons for the emotions they explain, in that way securing the view of justified emotions we have put forward. On the whole, this chapter will then emphasize the contrast between the reasons that merely explain why one has an emotion and the justificatory reasons for this emotion.

## Moods and temperaments

As we already observed in Chapter 1, moods and emotions are similar in being occurrent states with a salient phenomenology but differ as regards their intentionality. Emotions are always about particular objects, whereas moods are not. While we have seen that emotions are specific evaluative attitudes we take towards particular objects, moods are not directed at particular objects and thus do not consist in evaluations of these objects. One is always angry at someone or something on this or that account, one is not grumpy at someone or something on this or that account. If Jonas's remark angers Michelle, it must be because Michelle has evaluated his remark as offensive. On the other hand, Michelle's grumpiness does not entail that she has taken any evaluative attitude towards anything at all. This is why it makes sense to ask whether Michelle's anger is correct or justified, but not to ask the same of her grumpiness.

To substantiate this point, we can observe that, although we can ask why-questions both about Michelle's anger and her grumpiness, the types of responses we expect are very different. In the former case, we expect to be provided with information that serves to justify the emotional attitude, whereas, in the latter case, we are satisfied when presented with a plausible causal story about the mood in question, a story that might for example make reference to a headache, a shortage of coffee, or the trail left by a previously experienced emotion. This distinctive position of moods in our fabric of explanatory relations is further attested by the fact that moods are never appealed to in order to justify emotions, but to excuse or to provide miti-gating circumstances when they seem to come out of the blue (Goldie 2000: 143–51). This explains why, when you are aware of a mood and its potential effects on your emotional responses, you should – and typically will – consider the presence of the mood as throwing doubt on the emotion's justification and correctness. Michelle might for instance say to Jonas 'Sorry for getting angry at you earlier, I was just grumpy.'

The point of these explanations, then, consists in presenting the emotion as unjustified given its source in the mood rather than in the relevant properties of its object. Michelle's grumpiness, as opposed to anything Jonas has said or done, explains why she ends up seeing his remark as offensive. The object and those of its properties that would have made the emotion justified do not play the relevant role in Michelle's evaluation, which is instead explained by her mood. As a result, her emotion is perceived as unjustified. Moods are typically disconnected from any evaluative outlook, and in this sense expla-nations in terms of moods can be said to constitute arational explanations of why emotions occur.[1]

Much the same is true when the presence of the mood is further explained by reference to the subject's temperament. But what are temperaments?

There are three main types of explanations of why moods occur. They may be caused by non-psychological factors, e.g., lack of caffeine, or by prior emotions, as when one is in an elated mood because one has received good news in the morning. The third type of explanation proceeds not by referring to previous mental or non-mental episodes, but to the subject's disposition to slip into certain moods, as when we explain Michelle's grumpiness by saying that she is of the irritable type. In so doing, we understand her mood by locating it in a recurring pattern of affective states of this nature; we point here to a stable disposition to experience grumpiness. More generally, by using expressions such as 'being irritable', 'phlegmatic' (inclination to be in calm or relaxed moods), 'melancholic' (depressed or downcast), or 'lascivious' (aroused), we seem to be in the business of explaining the occurrence of moods by means of dispositions to enter into such states. In all these cases, it is correct to say that we refer to dispositions to enter into distinctive internal climates or tempers, which is exactly what the term 'temperament' appears to capture. The language of temperaments thus serves to provide an additional layer of explanation that connects with moods. This link between temperaments and moods is obvious when it is observed that the role of temperaments in psychological explanation is very similar to that played by moods. Temperaments figure prominently in arational explanations of emotions, and provide excuses or mitigating circumstances rather than justification for them.

Thus, when moods and temperaments explain the occurrence of emotions, they serve to set aside the possibility that the emotions in question are justified. Later in this chapter, we shall inquire whether the negative impact of moods and temperaments on the epistemological quality of our emotions threatens the account of justified emotions we offered in Chapter 8. For now, let us turn our attention to character traits.

## Character traits and sentiments

In the spirit of a long tradition of thinking about the virtues, we shall defend the claim that explanations in terms of character traits serve to draw attention to the specificities of a subject's emotional profile reflecting her broader evaluative outlook. This account will shed light on the following paradigmatic examples of character traits: being optimistic, kind, courteous, opportunist, meticulous, modest, loyal, frivolous, cruel, but also negligent, insensitive, unfriendly as well as the standard virtues and vices.

Character traits, in a nutshell, are ways of connecting in a *stable* and *coherent* way two dimensions of a subject's psychology: a cognitive and a conative dimension (e.g., Hudson 1980). Consider kindness and cruelty. When we call someone kind, we characterize her as manifesting on the one hand a tendency to apprehend situations in terms of the presence of others in need of help (cognitive dimension) and on the other hand as being motivated to help those she apprehends as being in need of help (conative dimension). Similarly, when we characterize a person as cruel, we think of her as prone to evaluate situations in terms of opportunities to make others suffer (cognitive dimension) and as motivated to inflict suffering (conative dimension). And note that it would be strange to call someone kind or cruel if any one of these dimensions is lacking.

Now, one might think that kind and cruel people make the same cognitive assessments of the situations they confront and only differ as regards their respective conative attitudes vis-à-vis these situations. Both are distinctively sensitive to the predicaments of others, but the former wants to help whereas the latter wants to cause further suffering. This should strike us as implausible, however: intuitively, kind and cruel people apprehend the presence of suffering in radically different ways. And there is little doubt that what explains our dissatisfaction with the above model is the intuition that kind and cruel people take very different affective attitudes towards the presence of suffering. That is to say, it appears wrong-headed to think that their respective cognitions differ only in that the information gleaned is used to satisfy opposite desires.

When thought of as manifestations of a character trait, the relevant cognitions must rather be understood in terms of different emotional attitudes that manifest radically divergent affective sensibilities. Kind and cruel people will for instance react to the actual presence of suffering through compassion and *Schadenfreude*, respectively. And, if the apprehension of the situation proceeds in terms of emotional attitudes, this means that the cognitive dimension of character traits is not motivationally neutral. Indeed, as we argued in Chapter 7, distinct emotional attitudes are distinct types of felt bodily stances. An emotion is an attitude towards a given situation or object that consists in being prepared to deal with it in a specific way. This is precisely why we should appeal to emotional attitudes to understand the intimate link between the cognitive and conative dimensions of character traits.

So, the crucial question is the following one: what gets added when we explain a given emotional attitude (e.g., compassion) by a character trait (e.g., kindness)? To explain an episode of compassion by mentioning the person's kindness is not only to say that the presence of suffering made her feel compassion or that she tends to feel it in such circumstances. Reference to a character trait is more informative than that and consists in locating this emotion in a much broader affective sensitivity. To claim that an episode of compassion has its source in kindness is to claim that this affective response is part of a larger pattern of real and counterfactual evaluations the subject either does make or would make in similar circumstances. For instance, we mean to convey that the presence of suffering will elicit the kind person's sympathy, other things being equal, that for her the likelihood of another's suffering will elicit dread that it will really occur, and the hope that it will not, that if nothing is done to relieve it, she will be likely to feel anger or indignation, that if she can do something about it and does it, relief may ensue, and that if she does not, she will likely feel guilt, remorse, or shame, etc. The fact that this affective structure is not likely to be shared by the cruel person, whose apprehension of suffering will connect with an entirely different set of potential or actual emotional responses, is what explains the intuition that cruel and kind people apprehend suffering in radically different ways. The claim, then, is that the mode of apprehension distinctive of character traits should be understood as essentially involving emotional responses.

Now, because explanations in terms of character traits connect with this deeply rooted complex fabric of affective dispositions, explaining an emotion, attendant behavior and habits of thought in terms of a character trait is to specify the weight or lack of weight subjects lend to specific values or disvalues (e.g., Wiggins 1975–76). Calling someone courteous or boastful is to say that she is distinctly sensitive to a certain value (say, respect and personal achievements) while calling her insensitive or negligent is to say that she is blind to other values. Within this picture, we can now understand what it means to say that explanations in terms of character traits point to a certain *stability* and *coherence* in a subject's emotional responses. Indeed, either the character traits will manifest themselves straightforwardly in the typical behavior associated with the trait (helping, making suffer) – this constitutes their stability – or, when they cannot express themselves, they manifest themselves, as we have just illustrated, in specific future-, present-, or past-oriented emotions; this is the aforementioned coherence. The reasons for which they may not manifest themselves straightforwardly will of course be of many different types. The cruel person might also be opportunistic, or simply have had a wonderful day, facts that might prevent him from manifesting his cruelty by cruel behavior. That is to say, traits operate neither in isolation from one another, nor in isolation from other motives, any of which might take, and often do take, precedence over a given trait.[2]

Character traits should now be contrasted with an important class of affective phenomena, sentiments, that are, in many respects, very similar to them and have the same explanatory role. The relevant difference is that, whereas character traits are attachments to values, the affective phenomena that will interest us now constitute attachments to specific things, typically people, but also animals, artifacts, and institutions. Love and hate are the paradigmatic forms of these attachments and this is why, following a venerable use of the term, we shall refer to attachments and aversions of these sorts as 'sentiments' (e.g., Broad 1954: 212–14, Frijda 2007: 192–93). Sentiments come in many different forms. The affection you may have for your hamster, your devotion to your country, your dislike of the banking establishment, and your great fondness for the most recent electronic gadgets all exhibit the required structure to qualify as sentiments. Sentiments are often traceable to repeated emotional interactions with their objects, an ebb and flow of episodes, which through a process of sedimentation settles into distinctive long-standing affective orientations towards them (e.g., Broad 1954: 297–98).

As with character traits, explanations in terms of sentiments also serve to connect in a stable and coherent fashion a cognitive and a motivational dimension of a subject's psychology. On the cognitive side, ascriptions of sentiments go hand in hand with dispositions to make distinctive evaluations of the situations involving the object of the sentiment. A lover will for instance apprehend situations involving her beloved in a way not shared by those lacking her sentiment. In the most abstract terms, she will evaluate positively situations that positively affect her beloved, and evaluate negatively situations that negatively affect him. Of course, the reverse will be the case if she hates rather than loves him. On the motivational side, we conceive of someone with a given sentiment as having a specific motivational structure: the lover is motivated to further the beloved's interests, to help him when in need, to act in the beloved's interests even when they conflict with hers, etc. Meanwhile the person filled with hatred will want to inflict pain, even when this conflicts with her own interests, etc.

This means that, like character traits, sentiments explain by ascribing a stability and coherence in the weight subjects assign to specific kinds of reasons in their feelings and attendant behavior. Moreover, the relevant notion of weight can be cashed out in terms similar to those we used with respect to character traits. Sentiments are also dispositions to feel specific types of emotions in given actual or counterfactual circumstances. The lover apprehends the situations faced by the beloved through distinctive emotional attitudes that will not be shared by someone who hates or is indifferent. The desecration of his church will anger the devout in a way that might fill the infidel with joy. The fact that sentiments primarily connect with dispositions to experience emotions means that sentiments, like character traits, are distinctive kinds of evaluative sensitivities. In character traits, one is emotionally sensitive to the fortune of a particular value; in sentiments, one is emotionally sensitive to the fortune of a given object. While the honest person will feel uncomfortable or perhaps outraged at the presence of injustice, the father will rejoice or perhaps feel pride at the success of his daughter.[3]

A fundamental contrast between moods and temperaments, on the one hand, and character traits and sentiments, on the other, then emerges. We have seen that the explanation of an emotion in terms of the former is incompatible with its justification, since they set aside the possibility of the emotion being a response to an awareness of properties that could justify it. This is clearly not the case with character traits and sentiments. Although vices and some proclivities we have for certain values and objects may indeed explain why we undergo unjustified emotions, there is no reason to think that sentiments and character traits systematically prevent us from responding to those properties that justify the emotions we experience. When we ascribe character traits and sentiments to people, we are drawing attention to the weight they lend to a given value or object, and this does not in itself constitute a negative epistemological verdict regarding the emotions thereby explained. Let us now complete our survey of a subject's motivational set and its role in explaining his emotions by saying a few words about desires.

## Desires

At the end of our discussion in Chapter 3, we suggested that we should conceive of desires in a restricted manner, namely as states that fix aims for the subject. More specifically, we endorsed a conception of desires on which they aim at being fulfilled, i.e. are inclinations to bring about changes in the world so that the world comes to be as it is represented in these desires. This is why, we said, it always makes sense to regard desires as states that can be satisfied or frustrated. And we shall now understand why desires are, as we suggested at the end of Chapter 3 and at various points in Chapter 7, attitudes that also have correctness conditions: they are correct when the desired state of affairs is something that ought to obtain (or, on a narrower conception we alluded to, something the subject ought to bring about). We shall unpack this insight by examining the explanatory relations between emotions and desires conceived of as very distinct types of mental states.

As we already stressed, desires stand in multifarious and important relations to the emotions. We often explain desires in terms of emotions, as when we say that John wants to climb up the tree because he is afraid of the bear. And we also often cite desires in order to explain why emotions occur, as when we observe that Marcella is happy to bump into John because she wanted to meet him. Let us consider this latter kind of explanation from an epistemological standpoint.

Explanations of emotions in terms of desires clearly differ from explanations in terms of moods and temperaments because they do not set aside the possibility that the emotions they explain are justified. The fact that Marcella's joy is explained by her desire to meet John certainly does not show that it is thereby unjustified. Generally speaking, such explanations are perfectly compatible with the emotions being justified. In some cases, it is true, the fact that an emotion is explained by a desire suggests that it is not justified. This can likely be traced back to the specific etiology and content of the desire as well as to its function in the circumstances. One may for instance wake up with a desire to smack someone, a desire for which one has no reason at all and which is completely disconnected from one's evaluative outlook, yet feel joy instead of shame or guilt as a result of having satisfied it.

Desires that we use to explain emotions need not be unmotivated in this way, however. More often than not, our desires have a given content because of some reason we have to favor or disfavor a specific course of action, i.e. they are themselves reason-responsive states or, as they are sometimes called, motivated desires (e.g., Nagel 1970: Chapter 5, Platts 1991, Schueler 1995: Chapter 1). Marcella may for instance have formed the desire to visit John because she read what he wrote and came to think positively of him. More generally, motivated desires are typically explained by underlying sentiments and character traits. Marcella's desire to visit John is explained by the fact that she likes him, i.e. a sentiment of hers that motivates her to pursue the relevant course of action and that is correct when her visiting him is a state of affairs that ought to obtain. Motivated desires represent in this sense what ought to obtain given the weight one assigns to certain values or objects. The sense in which these desires are correct or incorrect, then, can be traced back to the correctness or incorrectness of the evaluative states that motivate them, and to whether the state of affairs desired indeed ought to obtain (or is what the subject ought to bring about) given the various ends these values and objects may fix for the subject. Moreover, it is worth noticing here that this conclusion mirrors the one we reached at the end of the previous chapter: it is always by reference to an evaluative property that we explain why a norm applies in any given circumstances. It is for instance because the painting is beautiful that one ought to desire seeing it.

To return to the object of our present inquiry, observe that since motivated desires stand in the above-mentioned explanatory relations to sentiments and character traits, we should reach conclusions regarding explanations of emotions that proceed in terms of such desires, identical to those we reached with respect to explanations of them that directly proceed in terms of sentiments and character traits. The fact that Marcella's joy at finally meeting John is explained by this motivated desire of hers is, in itself, epistemologically neutral.

These observations on the explanatory relations existing between desires, character traits, and sentiments put us in an ideal position to come back to the conclusion we reached in Chapter 3 regarding the nature of what we have called 'desires with open contents', those desires, such as the desire to preserve one's life or to see works of art, that we said explain the occurrence of emotions insofar as they are states of valuing. Now, we may think of ascriptions of desires of this kind as ascriptions of more or less inchoate collections of aims the subject inclines to attain – collections of what we have called 'desires with restricted contents'. If so, these are indeed desires as we have characterized them throughout this book. The present discussion, however, suggests a different conclusion. It is fair to say that, when we explain the occurrence of an emotion by an open desire, we do not merely allude to the various states of affairs a subject may be inclined to bring about; rather, we explain her emotion by pointing to what she values, positively or negatively. The same is true, we submit, of many explanations of emotions in terms of wishes (de Sousa 1987: 169). It is for instance because you value your life that you feel afraid in given circumstances. And it should now be clear that these states of valuing are not desires, but rather affective sensitivities to some objects or values, i.e. sentiments or character traits. Indeed, while it makes sense to say that they can motivate states that fix aims for the subject, i.e. motivated desires, they do not, in and of themselves, aim at being fulfilled.

Thus, depending on the sorts of desires (motivated or unmotivated) that explanations of emotions appeal to, the nature of the explanation will differ. Reference to a desire, as with reference to a character trait or a sentiment, rarely constitutes a negative epistemological verdict regarding the emotion it explains. Still, the very existence of motivational states that are detrimental to the justification of the emotions they explain may seem to threaten the soundness of the account of justified emotions put forward in Chapter 8. Our next task is then to assess whether these threats have any substance to them.

## Limits on the negative epistemological role of motivational states

We have remarked that moods, temperaments, as well as some character traits, sentiments, and desires, are likely to have distorting effects on our emotional lives. Love may spawn unwarranted admiration, and anger may stem from grumpiness or irascibility rather than from anything that would justify it. The worry now is that these phenomena are so pervasive that they threaten our account of justified emotions, an account that presupposes that emotions reliably track evaluative properties. After all, if motivational states do constantly distort our emotional responses, this would turn any occasion on which an emotion is experienced in the presence of the relevant evaluative properties into no more than a lucky event, something widely agreed to be incompatible with justification (e.g., Pritchard 2005). Do we have reason to think that the existence of distorting motivational states has such dramatic consequences, however? To borrow Goldie's apt phrase, do they systematically 'skew the evaluative landscape' (Goldie 2004b)?

First, let us observe that, if motivational states did always distort our apprehension of the evaluative domain, this would have serious skeptical consequences. For we know that when motivational states exert distorting effects, these effects are not confined to our emotional responses, but also affect the way we rationalize these responses and, more generally, a wide range of evaluative judgments (e.g., Elster 1999: Chapter 5, Goldie 2008, Nisbett and Ross 1980). The potentially distorting effects of love extend well beyond the mere eliciting of unwarranted emotions like admiration, to influencing our judgments about there being reasons to admire and, more generally, to insinuating themselves into evaluations of various objects. So, if motivational states with such damaging effects are ever-present, this would deprive us of any safe access to the evaluative domain. And this skeptical conclusion can only be resisted if the above epistemological consequences only pertain to problematic motivational states: not all of them prove detrimental to the idea that emotions can be justified along the lines we recommend.[4]

Second, and in close connection to the point just made, the significance of the present worry depends on how we demarcate the domain relevant for assessing whether an emotion manifests a capacity to reliably track the evaluative facts. This is an instance of what epistemologists call the 'generality problem' (e.g., Conee and Feldman 1998). Consider anger, and suppose that you are angry at a sexually offensive remark. For your emotion to be justified, should it manifest a capacity to track sexual offensiveness, the offensive in general, or a more extended domain of evaluative facts? You may after all only be able to reliably track the first property. And if, for a given emotion to be justified, it is required that the reliability of the tracking ability extends well beyond the type of case at hand, then justified emotions may be hard to come by. Yet it is difficult to see why such a requirement would apply to the justification of any given emotion. Why think for instance that one's competence in tracking slight-to-honor-based offenses is relevant for assessing the reliability of an emotion responding to the sexually offensive? And if the requirement concerning reliable tracking applies for that reason to a more limited domain, then the answer to the present worry should proceed in a careful, piecemeal fashion, i.e. by considering whether, say, the subject's emotion manifests a capacity to track the sexually offensive in a variety of contexts.

For these reasons, the fact that some of our emotions are biased by the presence of distorting motivational states does not imply that, when our emotions respond to properties apt to justify them, this is no more than a lucky event.

## A positive epistemological role for motivational states?

We have seen that some motivational states are incompatible with the justification of emotions. This leaves quite open the central question we shall now address: whether motivational states can positively contribute to the justification of emotions. In other words, when sentiments, character traits, and desires do not play a distorting effect, do they merely locate the emotion in the subject's broader evaluative outlook, or do they in addition constitute justificatory reasons for the emotions they explain? Do the facts that kindness explains an episode of compassion, that one's love for a child explains the pride at her achievement, or that one's desire to meet someone explains the joy one feels upon meeting this person constitute justificatory reasons for these emotions?

In Chapter 8, we defended the idea that emotions are justified if, and only if, in the circumstances in which she finds herself, the subject is (or seems to be) aware of properties that (would) constitute specific instances of the evaluative properties that make these emotions correct. One might think that such an exclusive focus on the properties of the object in justifying the emotions cannot be right, given the constant appeal to motivational states in explaining them. Surely, these states must also, in one way or another, play a positive epistemological role. Now, while quite intuitive, this thought is difficult to substantiate. In our opinion, there are two different ways of doing so.

First, one may think that motivational states contribute positively to justification, because emotions in fact inherit their justified or unjustified character from that of these motivational states. We have seen that some motivational states – one's sadistic tendencies, say – undermine the justification of the emotions they explain – one's joy in someone's suffering. According to the present idea, this is because these states are themselves unjustified. So why not think that when emotions are justified, this is partly because the motivational states that explain them are justified? The idea would be that Mark's pride in the fact that this little girl has won the prize is not only explained by his love for her, but that the justification of his emotion is inherited from the justification of his love. Similarly, fear is justified to the extent that the concern for one's physical integrity that explains it is justified.

The first observation to make is that this view puts some severe constraints on the nature of character traits, sentiments, and those desires that may justify emotions. They cannot be conceived, as they commonly are, as dispositions individuated in terms of their manifestations, among which emotional episodes are central. For, if dispositions (or their categorical bases) can explain their manifestations, this explanation does not seem to carry any justificatory implication. For instance, judgments that P are amongst the manifestations of the belief that P and someone's believing that P can surely explain his judging that P. Yet, the belief that P cannot justify the judgment that P; it is simply not a reason in favor of this judgment. This carries over to the relation between motivational states and emotions, insofar as we think of the former as being merely dispositions to undergo emotions. The nature of this relation is simply incompatible with the claim that emotions inherit their justification from that of the motivational states they manifest.

This means that, in order to say that there are justificatory relations between character traits, sentiments, desires, and emotions, one must, quite controversially, conceive of the former not merely as dispositions to undergo the latter, but rather as something like long-lasting affective states that are independent of the emotions to which they give rise. Mark's love for his niece is now viewed as a long-standing intentional relation to her that can be justified only if there is evidence that she is indeed loveable. One must also claim that the emotions to which these states give rise – an episode of pride at his niece's achievement, say – inherit their justification from that of these states.

The plausibility of this view depends on its ability to build a case against the following intuitions. First, not only do many of our motivational states seem, as we have suggested, to emerge from a series of emotions about their object, but the justification of the former seems also to depend on that of the latter. Intuitively, it makes more sense to say that my love for all things Shakespearian inherits its justification from the many specific and distinct justified emotional experiences his works have elicited in me, and out of which my love has emerged, than the other way around. Second, the advocate of this view will have to explain away the intuition that many emotions – like the admiration one may feel on discovering an artist's work – do not seem to be accounted for by any long-standing intentional relation (see Chapter 3) and *a fortiori* by one from which they can inherit their own justification.

If these challenges can be met, then we have one reason to conceive of motivational states as positively contributing to the justification of emotions. But this is not the only one. An alternative way of fleshing out this proposal consists in arguing that motivational states partly or wholly constitute the evaluative properties to which emotions respond (e.g., Helm 2001). For instance, one's desire to preserve one's physical integrity should be counted amongst the properties that constitute a specific danger in the light of which a given episode of fear is justified and one's concern for one's honor partly constitutes the sort of degradation in the light of which shame is justified. Because the relevant motivational states partly constitute the evaluative properties to which emotions respond, one is justified in responding with a given emotion only insofar as one is in the relevant motivational state.

It is fair to say that the subjectivist view on the nature of evaluative properties that supports this conclusion, and that we had the occasion to criticize in Chapter 4, is at least as controversial as the view about the nature of motivational states we have just examined. Let us simply observe that, although why-questions about the emotions are often answered by reference to motivational states, this fact does nothing to support this subjectivism. These answers appear to have the function of explaining why the relevant emotion occurs rather than that of explaining why it is justified or correct. This is especially clear in all those cases we have discussed in which motivational states are conscripted into explanations of why unjustified emotions occur.

We have assessed two ways of supporting the idea that motivational states positively contribute to the justification of emotions, and have argued that neither is without problems. This strongly suggests in our opinion that, even when motivational states are perfectly compatible with the justification of emotions, they do not yield justificatory reasons in their favor. Explaining emotions by means of these states has the function of rooting them in a broader evaluative outlook that helps us see the weight or lack of weight subjects lend to specific values or objects. And note that understanding the role of motivational states as exclusively explanatory will block any motivation one might have to think that the subject must be aware of them, as he must be aware of the cognitive base of his emotion according to our account. Given that they play no justificatory role, there seems to be no reason for requiring that the subject be aware of these motivational states.[5] This is good news for the account on offer, for, on the face of it, there seems to be no reason to think that, if Mark's pride over his niece's achievement is to be justified, he must be aware of his love for her, or be able to articulate that love. After all, even if his pride came as a total surprise to him, this would still not carry the implication that it is unjustified. For these reasons, the analysis of justified emotions put forward in Chapter 8 need not be amended to accommodate the role played by the emotions' motivational bases.

## Conclusion

In this chapter, we sought to neutralize worries surrounding our account of justified emotions in relation to the fact that we constantly feel the need to explain their occurrence by reference to the subject's motivational set. We saw that moods, temperaments, character traits, sentiments, and desires provide distinct types of affective explanations. While pointing to such states sometimes serves to depict the emotions they explain as unjustified, we concluded that doing so never consists in pointing to justificatory reasons for these emotions.

## Questions and further readings

(1)    What are the main differences between explanations in terms of moods and temperaments on the one hand, and explanations in terms of character traits and sentiments on the other hand?
(2)    Why should we resist the thought that the epistemological standing of emotions is systematically threatened by motivational states?
(3)    Do motivational states contribute to the justification of emotions? If not, why?

Essentially conative accounts of *character traits* are defended in Brandt (1982) and Harman (1999), while Hudson (1980) emphasizes their two-dimensional (cognitive and conative) nature. The claim that these two dimensions of character traits are independent from one another is made salient in Butler (1988). On the idea that character traits and sentiments are to be understood in terms of the *weight* given to distinct reasons or values, see McDowell (1979), Morton (1980), and Wiggins (1975–76). For a detailed analysis of this notion of weight in terms of holistic and dynamical affective structures, see Helm (2001) and especially Helm (2010) for what we call sentiments. A very nice general introduction to the nature of *affective dispositions* is Goldie (2004a), while Schueler (2003: 69–88) provides a good discussion of character traits in the context of action explanation.

The question of whether *desires* broadly understood can constitute justificatory reasons has been typically and extensively addressed in connection with the explanation of action, and more specifically moral action. Useful defenses of the idea that they can play such a justificatory role can be found in Smith's (1994) classic discussion and, more recently, in Schroeder (2007). Helpful although difficult expositions and endorsements of the opposite claim are proffered by Dancy (1993) and Schueler (2003).

## Notes

1    None of this implies that moods cannot constitute reasons when they feature in the content of other mental states. A prolonged mood may for instance worry me. The mood is here the object of my worry, and may in itself constitute a reason to worry.
2    The fact that character traits do not operate in isolation provides the resources for countering the widespread skepticism regarding the very existence of character traits (see Doris 2002). For discussions of why this skepticism is not warranted, see Deonna and Teroni (2009) and Goldie (2000, 2004a).
3    In Chapter 1, we distinguished not only character traits and sentiments but also emotional dispositions such as one's disposition to fear dogs or hate bodybuilders. These may be

single-track dispositions to feel the emotion towards the relevant objects. But, typically, we believe, they should be understood either in terms of character traits or in terms of sentiments, depending on whether the emphasis is put on the particular objects themselves, or on the values the subject takes them to exemplify. For a detailed analysis, see Deonna and Teroni (2009).

4  These observations of course raise an important question in relation to the evaluative judgments we reach as a result of having an emotion. Should we require of the subject that she makes sure that distorting affective factors do not bias the emotion on which her judgment is based? This is a topic we shall address in the final chapter.

5  Note that even if motivational states did play a positive epistemological role vis-à-vis emotions, this would not as such imply that they are subject to an accessibility requirement. Insisting on such a requirement would be to overlook a familiar and important contrast, that between justification and the capacity to articulate the reasons why one is justified. For a discussion of this issue, see Deonna and Teroni (2012).

# 10 The importance of emotions

Emotions are attitudes that depend epistemologically on the content of the states that function as their cognitive bases. This is true even though a variety of motivational states are sometimes or perhaps always amongst the determinants of our emotional responses. As we have seen, securing this sort of epistemological dependence constitutes the way in which the attitudinal theory presented in Chapter 7 meets the first part of our epistemological constraint. In this final chapter, we want to show how it meets the second part of this constraint: the idea that emotions constitute privileged sources of justification for the evaluative judgments they explain. We have seen that emotions can and typically do give rise to evaluative judgments: John judges that the joke is funny because he is amused by it, Mary judges the remark to be offensive because she is angry at its author. Yet, are these emotions, in addition, apt to justify these judgments they so often explain? We first inquire whether the emotions can constitute sufficient grounds for making justified evaluative judgments. We conclude that they can and then argue that they even constitute a privileged epistemological route for our knowledge of value.

## From justified emotions to justified evaluative judgments

The natural thought at this stage of our discussion is the following. Whatever it is that justifies an emotion, i.e. the specific content of the emotion's cognitive base, should also suffice to justify the corresponding evaluative judgment. That is to say, given the situation in which the subject finds herself, if the content of her awareness justifies fear or anger towards an object, then her judging on the basis of this same content that the object is, respectively, dangerous or offensive would also be justified (see Goldie 2004b for the same conclusion). Things might not be as straightforward as they seem, however.

There may be constraints weighing on justified evaluative judgments that do not apply to justified emotions. One key idea, one that already surfaced a few times in this book (Chapter 7, p. 84, Chapter 8, pp. 100–101) is that evaluative concepts are concepts of appropriate emotions. To judge that something is dangerous, amusing, or constitutes a loss is to judge that fear, amusement, or sadness, respectively, would be appropriate (e.g., D'Arms 2005, McDowell

1985). Yet, as you will remember, neither the subject's awareness of the situation (awareness, say, of a dog with sharp teeth), nor his having the emotion (fearing the dog) is identical to awareness that it is appropriate to have it: emotions cannot refer to their own appropriateness in that way (Brady 2010). This suggests that justified emotions cannot by themselves justify the corresponding evaluative judgments, and that the subject thus needs to ascertain, in one way or another, that the emotion she experiences does indeed suit the situation she is facing (e.g., Jones 2006). Now, the idea that the subject needs to ascertain that her emotion fits the situation can be pursued in at least two directions. First, the suggestion may be that she must rule out any involvement of the kinds of distorting factors in her response that we discussed in Chapter 9 in connection with motivational states. Second, and perhaps more fundamentally, the idea may be that she must, given the nature of the evaluative concepts featuring in her judgment, make sure that her emotion is appropriate in the circumstances. Let us take these issues in turn.

As regards the first suggestion, it is clear that there are circumstances in which the making of a justified evaluative judgment requires that the subject take into account her present conative or emotional state. If Suzanne is very downcast because of some bad news she has just heard, her emotional responses may no doubt be distorted as a result. In such a case, the judgments she may make on the basis of her emotions can still be justified, but only if she can establish that it is not her downcast condition that is at the root of her emotions. This kind of example shows that some circumstances do indeed require the subject to take into account the fact that her emotions do not constitute safe grounds for the corresponding evaluative judgments. They do not show, however, that such a requirement holds each time we make this kind of judgment on the basis of our emotions. Similarly, there are some circumstances in which justified color judgments must take into account occasional bizarre or distorting lighting conditions, but this does not support the idea that justified color judgments made in more favorable conditions also require that the subject make sure the conditions are not unfavorable. So, this first suggestion provides no reason to think that emotions cannot be sufficient to justify the corresponding evaluative judgments.

Let us now turn to the second suggestion. Suppose that making an evaluative judgment does indeed involve the tacit implication that a given emotion would be appropriate. Does this entail that a justified emotion is insufficient for the corresponding judgment's justification, i.e. for justifiably judging that this emotion is appropriate? It is far from obvious that this is so. A justified emotion, we have said, is one that is based on (real or apparent) awareness of properties that, in the circumstances, (would) constitute an instance of the relevant evaluative property. When you respond emotionally to these properties in the absence of any reason to think the response is incorrect or otherwise misleading, you seem to be in a position to justifiably judge that these properties are exemplified and so to justifiably make the corresponding evaluative judgment. To put it differently, the difficulty fades away once we remind ourselves (see Chapter 4, pp. 48–49 and Chapter 8, p. 101) that the predicate 'justified' means, when applied to the emotions, what it is customarily taken to mean in other areas of discourse, namely that there are good and undefeated reasons to take the facts as these emotions do. It is precisely in virtue of the existence of these reasons that the corresponding evaluative judgments deem these emotions appropriate.

Hence, even if evaluative concepts are concepts of appropriate emotions, this does not support the conclusion that justified emotions are insufficient for justified evaluative judgments. Yet consider the following line of thought. Given what we have said so far, making an evaluative judgment would seem to consist in committing oneself to there being reasons to think an evaluative property is exemplified. Making a justified evaluative judgment would then require having good reasons to think that this is so. So, under what circumstances does one have sufficient reasons to commit oneself in this way? And here it may be suggested: only when one can articulate what features of the situation render the judgment that the value is exemplified reasonable. It now seems as if having a justified emotion does not in itself put one in a position to achieve that much. Suppose for instance that Jim rushes out of a conference room claiming that the situation was deeply embarrassing. His judgment is explained, for instance, by the justified embarrassment he felt, which responded to various subtle clues in the audience. As he is making his judgment, however, he is unable to specify the relevant features. The suggestion is that, given the above-mentioned constraint, his inability invalidates his judgment, and this then shows that justified emotions are at least sometimes not sufficient for the justification of the corresponding evaluative judgment. Should we accept this conclusion?

The following observations suggest we should not. In the light of the foregoing considerations, we should favor the following approach. The mere occurrence of emotions is not sufficient to justify corresponding evaluative judgments: only *justified* emotions, whose justification depends on the nature of their bases, are sufficient. Applied to Jim's case, the idea is that, given that awareness of the relevant cues justifies his embarrassment, his judgment that the situation is embarrassing would be justified *if based on awareness of the same cues*. The fact that these cues are not accessible when he is out of the room and making his evaluative judgment is beside the point, since his emotion would also be unjustified if it were to take place in the same circumstances, i.e. absent any awareness of good reasons.

These observations lead us to conclude that justified emotions are sufficient to justify evaluative judgments. What our discussion of the present worry has brought out is that if one conceives of evaluative concepts as concepts of appropriate emotional responses, then it is indeed difficult to conceive of the mastery of these concepts as independent of a general ability to articulate the sorts of conditions that can distinguish justified from unjustified emotions. The fact that this is the case, however, should not be taken as showing that an emotion responding to properties in virtue of which it is justified is insufficient to warrant the application of the relevant evaluative concept. This is true even though the subject would not make the judgment if he had not acquired the relevant conceptual ability. Here again, considering the case of perception is helpful. Perceptual experiences we have no reason to distrust – perception, say, of an oak tree in broad daylight – are sufficient to justify perceptual judgments (e.g., 'this is green') even though the subject would not have made these judgments if he had not acquired the relevant conceptual abilities (e.g., Pollock and Cruz 1999: Chapter 2).

Now, if justified emotions are sufficient for justified evaluative judgments, do they constitute a privileged route for the making of these judgments and hence for our knowledge of value? It is to this final issue that we turn.

## Emotions and emotional sensitivity

The idea that justified emotions constitute a privileged epistemological route for making justified evaluative judgments – namely the second part of our epistemological constraint – is at first sight in serious tension with the idea, which lies at the center of our account, that emotions and evaluative judgments are justified by the same reasons. After all, if the content of one's awareness justifies an emotion, then it would have justified the corresponding evaluative judgment even though one did not experience the emotion. This is because a justified evaluative judgment is always 'in principle inferable' from the information available to the subject independently of his emotion (Peacocke 2004: 258). Now, the existence of two routes to justified evaluative judgments, an emotional one and a route bypassing emotions altogether, is in our opinion beyond dispute. Fortunately, we do not need to go through full-blown emotional experiences each time we make justified evaluative judgments.

What we shall dispute is the conclusion one may then be tempted to draw, namely that emotions are always epistemologically superfluous. Indeed, there are at least two reasons why we should not read too much into the idea that justified evaluative judgments are always, in principle, inferable independently of the corresponding emotions. First, our awareness of the properties that justify our evaluative judgments must often be explained by our emotional sensitivity. Second, the idea that emotions are epistemologically superfluous runs afoul of some plausible requirements on the understanding of evaluative judgments. Let us consider these in turn.

For an evaluative judgment to be justified, the subject must be sensitive to properties that function as reasons in its favor. And, while these properties can in principle be accessed by the subject independently of his emotions, it often proves difficult to see how he could access them without the relevant emotional sensitivity, i.e. his dispositions, variously shaped by his idiosyncratic developmental path, sentiments, character traits, and desires, to react emotionally to his surroundings. Given the complexity of the environment through which we navigate, the prospects for detecting properties that could justify evaluative judgments without the aid of such a sensitivity are not promising. As has been often observed, our distinct emotional sensitivities engender specific patterns of salience among the objects of our experience (e.g., de Sousa 1987: 195). Imagine for instance the task faced by a subject deprived of any sense of the comical, and required to latch on to what may be funny in any given conversation. Or consider the subtle cues (the way others look at us, which values are at stake in the circumstances, their relative importance, etc.) to which our sense of shame so often responds. As we have seen just above when considering the case of Jim, we often prove quite bad at articulating the reasons to which our emotions are responding when or just after we experience them.

This last observation proves crucial for the issue at hand, for it suggests that the evaluative verdict the subject would reach independently of his emotion may fail to respond to the good reasons his emotion responds to. In these quite common situations, the subject is emotionally attuned to the relevant reasons, but the conclusion he reaches in his cold hours fails (due to lack of intelligence, an ideological turn of mind, laziness, etc.) to envisage the relevant reasons as reasons, or to give them their due weight (Arpaly 2000). If, in such a situation, the subject makes the corresponding evaluative judgment on the basis of his emotion, perhaps with a sense that he should refrain from so judging, his judgment may well be justified despite his conflicting verdict reached through cool reflection. There may be different ways of developing these observations, one of which would consist in saying that the subject's judgment is justified if, absent the factors clouding his cooly reached conclusion, he would realize that the reasons his emotion responds to override his reasons to judge otherwise. The important point seems to be that there are evaluative judgments whose justification resists conflicting verdicts reached through cool reflection, because the emotions that explain them respond to good reasons.

This being the case, the fact that justified evaluative judgments are in principle inferable from the information available to the subject independently of his emotions does not support the conclusion that emotions are epistemologically superfluous (Peacocke 2004: 263–65). Far from it: good reasons for evaluative judgments may be in principle accessible independently of emotions, yet their relevance for these judgments would be missed or distorted if one were to coldly ponder the situation. As a result, the justification of these judgments can only be due to the fact that they are based on emotions responding to good reasons.

## Emotions and understanding

Of course, all this is compatible with the idea that an ideal observer may be in a position to reach justified evaluative judgments by exclusively following the non-emotional route. Yet we may want to deny that this is the case by appealing to a second reason for which emotions may be deemed epistemologically fundamental: being a competent user of evaluative concepts may after all require more than the mere ability to apply them in the correct circumstances. Categorizing an object as funny or shameful is indeed hardly detachable from the understanding that its properties give one reasons to favor or reject it. And we might wonder what sort of understanding of there being reasons to favor or reject an object we would preserve, were we deprived of the relevant emotions. Recall that emotions, as we have claimed in Chapter 7, are experiential attitudes that consist in one's readiness to act in various and distinctive ways vis-à-vis given objects or situations. And, if they are justified, then they allow us to experience the attitudes these objects or situations make appropriate. This is why, or so we have suggested, emotions prove to be intimately interwoven with our evaluative concepts: it is by experiencing the former that we come to be aware of the canonical conditions of application pertaining to the latter (Peacocke 1996, Zagzebski 2003, and Chapter 8).

The force of this point comes to light if we imagine a creature deprived of emotional responses who has been able to get a handle on our evaluative practices because, say, she has learned to recognize the responses of others. This creature is thus linking her application of evaluative concepts to responses she can discriminate correctly in others. But does she understand the evaluative judgments she makes? For her, judging that something is amusing, degrading, or offensive consists in realizing that the object's properties justify the amusement, shame, or anger of others. While her evaluative verdicts are in line with ours, the canonical conditions of application of her evaluative concepts are radically different from ours. She no doubt understands something, but not, we may think, the point of our evaluative practices. Her lack of emotional responses means that she cannot experience objects as giving her reasons to act in various and distinctive ways. Being deprived of the capacity to experience situations as offensive, shameful, or amusing for herself, the sense in which we may think of her as animated by concerns, such as staying decent, acting honorably, or cultivating her sense of humor, is elusive to say the least. She does not have any personal concern for staying decent, behaving honorably, or cultivating her sense of humor. Although she might succeed in blending in, as it were, such concerns could only be those of the people on whose responses she models her evaluative competence. If there is any point for her in making evaluative judgments, it is simply not the same as ours.

And note finally that her impairment may be even more severe, for many of our evaluative judgments are justified by facts pertaining to the course of other people's emotions ('this was the cruel thing to do', 'that was generous, they won't suffer anymore'). These evaluative judgments respond to the fact that we are emotional creatures, and a failure to have any experiential access to how given circumstances tend to emotionally impinge on us should make us wonder what a non-emotional creature can understand of the evaluative verdicts she comes up with.

Of course, we should not jump too hastily from considerations pertaining to concept possession and understanding to conclusions pertaining to epistemology and justification. Our subject, devoid of emotional experiences, will by hypothesis come up with evaluative judgments that reliably fit the evaluative facts, and this is enough to satisfy respectable models of what justification consists in. That being said, we should take the full measure of what this entails. It would amount to claiming that the sort of justification at play here is completely divorced from the kind of understanding that is implied by our evaluative practices, one that is constitutively connected to our emotional engagement with the world. This, then, is a second reason for thinking that emotions constitute an epistemologically privileged route for our knowledge of value.

## Conclusion

In this final chapter, we argued that emotions and evaluative judgments are justified by the same reasons. We wondered whether this makes the emotional route to evaluative judgments epistemologically superfluous, and gave reasons for thinking that, on the contrary, we should rather favor the opposite conclusion. First, given the sort of access to the evaluative world afforded by the emotions, the emotional route may be thought to compare favorably with the pitfalls surrounding an exclusive use of our reasoning powers. Second, given that our evaluative practices are constitutively linked to our capacity to feel emotions, the sense in which one might be justified in making evaluative judgments when these are not supported by the capacity for emotions is elusive to say the least.

This is why we can safely conclude that the emotions constitute a privileged route to the knowledge of the evaluative properties that feature in their respective correctness conditions. Observe moreover how broad a swathe of evaluative properties this epistemological claim applies to. It covers all of those we had the opportunity to discuss throughout this book, including those pertaining to the moral sphere and disclosed to us through the emotional attitudes of compassion, shame, guilt, indignation, resentment, perhaps disgust, etc. A further question, then, concerns the links between the disclosures of these specific evaluative properties and the judgments as to the overall goodness or badness of the situations we confront. The ways in which these all-things-considered moral judgments are informed by, and perhaps partly grounded in, our specific emotional responses is the object of intense and fascinating debate in the contemporary literature on the foundations of morality. We hope that the territory explored in this book will have provided some of the important tools needed to make progress on the burning question around which these debates revolve.

## Questions and further readings

(1)  Why think that having an emotion is not sufficient grounds on which to make the corresponding evaluative judgments?

(2)   What is the epistemological significance of the existence of two distinct routes to our evaluative judgments?
(3)   Why think that emotions play a fundamental role in our knowledge of value?

Most of the further readings suggested in the section *epistemology in connection to the emotions* in Chapter 8 are relevant for the issues discussed in the present chapter.

Aside from de Sousa (1987), many have insisted on the role of emotions in generating *patterns of salience*, see e.g., Baier (2004) and Elgin (2008). Lance and Tanesini (2004) emphasize this role of emotions in the context of problem solving, while Robinson (2005: Chapter 2) does the same in connection with aesthetic experience. Faucher and Tappolet (2002) offer a detailed discussion of this issue in the specific case of fear.

The idea that emotional reasons can *trump reasons* reached via more deliberative means is explored through an illuminating treatment of Huckleberry Finn's behavior in Arpaly (2002). Relevant to this topic are Jones (2003), Tappolet (2003) and, more generally, the collection of essays in Stroud and Tappolet (2003).

Working within very different frameworks and pursuing different aims, Prinz (2006: 38–39) and Roberts and Wood (2007: 53–54) both emphasize the centrality of emotions to the acquisition of evaluative concepts, and more generally the *understanding of our evaluative practices*. This is also a fundamental theme in Wiggins's (1987) seminal article and in Zagzebski's (2003) insightful piece that connects with many issues addressed in this chapter. Brady (2011) presents some important reasons to conceive of the emotions as playing a more subservient role in relation to evaluative knowledge.

David Hume (1975) is often considered the ultimate source for the idea that our *moral judgments* are grounded in our emotional responses. Prinz (2007) offers an empirically informed approach to moral judgment in the Humean tradition. Accounts of normative judgment driven by evolutionary considerations, which make essential reference to the emotions, are to be found in Haidt (2003) and Nichols (2007). On the same topic but coming from the metaethical tradition, see Blackburn (1998) and Gibbard (1990). Goldie (2007) provides an important discussion of the justification of moral judgment from within emotion theory.

# Bibliography

Alvarez, M. (2010). *Kinds of Reasons: An Essay in the Philosophy of Action*. New York: Oxford University Press.

Aristotle (1994). *On Rhetoric: A Theory of Civic Discourse* (transl. by G. Kennedy). New York: Oxford University Press.

Armon-Jones, C. (1986). 'The Thesis of Constructionism'. In R. Harré (ed.), *The Social Construction of the Emotions* (pp. 32–56). Oxford: Oxford University Press.

Armstrong, D. (1968). *A Materialist Theory of the Mind*. London: Routledge.

Arpaly, N. (2000). 'On Acting Rationally Against One's Best Judgment'. *Ethics* 110, 488–513.

——(2002). 'Moral Worth'. *The Journal of Philosophy* 99.5, 223–45.

Aue, T. and Scherer, K. R. (2008). 'Appraisal-driven Somatovisceral Response Patterning: Effects of Intrinsic Pleasantness and Goal Conduciveness'. *Biological Psychology* 79, 158–64.

Audi, R. (1995). 'Memorial Justification'. *Philosophical Topics* 23.1, 31–45.

Averill, J. (1980). 'A Constructivist View of Emotion'. In R. Plutchik and H. Kellermann (eds.), *Emotion: Theory, Research and Experience* (pp. 305–39). New York: Academic Press.

Baier, A. (2004). 'Feelings that Matter'. In R. C. Solomon (ed.), *Thinking about Feeling: Contemporary Philosophers on Emotions* (pp. 200–13). New York: Oxford University Press.

Barrett, L. F. (2006). 'Emotions as Natural Kinds?'. *Perspectives on Psychological Science* 1, 28–58.

Bedford, E. (1957). 'Emotions'. *Proceedings of the Aristotelian Society* 57, 281–304.

Ben Ze'ev, A. (2000). *The Subtlety of Emotions*. Cambridge, Mass.: MIT Press.

Binet, A. (1910). 'Qu'est-ce qu'une émotion? Qu'est-ce qu'un acte intellectuel?'. *L'année psychologique* 17, 1–47.

Blackburn, S. (1998). *Ruling Passions: A Theory of Practical Reasoning*. New York: Oxford University Press.

Brady, M. (2010). 'Virtue, Emotion, and Attention'. *Metaphilosophy* 41.1–2, 115–31.

——(2011). 'Emotions, Perceptions and Reasons'. In C. Bagnoli (ed.), *Morality and the Emotions*. New York: Oxford University Press.

Brandt, R. (1982). 'The Structure of Virtue'. *Midwest Studies of Philosophy* 13, 64–82.

Brentano, F. (1889/1969). *The Origin of Our Knowledge of Right and Wrong*. London: Routledge & Kegan Paul.

Broad, C. D. (1954). 'Emotion and Sentiment'. In D. Cheeney (ed.), *Broad's Critical Essays in Moral Philosophy*. New York: George Allen & Unwin.

Brun, G., Doğuoğlu, U., and Kuenzle, D. (eds.) (2008). *Epistemology and Emotions*. Aldershot: Ashgate.

Bull, N. (1951/1968). *The Attitude Theory of Emotion*. New York and London: Johnson Reprint Corporation.

Butler, D. (1988). 'Character Traits in Explanation'. *Philosophy and Phenomenological Research* 49.2, 215–38.

Cannon, W. B. (1927). 'The James-Lange Theory of Emotions: A Critical Examination and an Alternative Theory'. *American Journal of Psychology* 39, 106–24.

Charland, L. (2002). 'The Natural Kind Status of Emotion'. *British Journal for the Philosophy of Science* 53, 511–37.

Claparède, E. (1928). 'Feelings and Emotions'. In M. L. Reymert (ed.), *Feelings and Emotions: The Wittenberg Symposium* (pp. 124–39). Worcester: Clark University Press.

Clark, A. (2005). 'Painfulness is Not a Quale'. In M. Aydede (ed.), *Pain: New Essays on Its Nature and the Methodology of Its Study* (pp. 177–97). Cambridge, MA: MIT Press.

Cobos, P., Sanchez, M., Garcia, C., Nieves Vera, M., and Vila, J. (2002). 'Revisiting the James versus Cannon Debate on Emotion: Startle and Autonomic Modulation in Patients with Spinal Cord Injuries'. *Biological Psychology* 61.3, 251–69.

Cochrane, T. (2009). 'Eight Dimensions for the Emotions'. *Social Science Information* 48.3, 379–420.

Colombetti, G. (2005). 'Appraising Valence'. *Journal of Consciousness Studies* 12.8–10, 103–26.

——(2007). 'Enactive Appraisal'. *Phenomenology and the Cognitive Sciences* 6.4, 527–546.

Conee, E. and Feldman, R. (1998). 'The Generality Problem for Reliabilism'. *Philosophical Studies* 89.1, 1–29.

Cosmides, L. and Tooby, J. (2000). 'Evolutionary Psychology and the Emotions'. In M. Lewis and J. M. Haviland-Jones (eds.), *Handbook of Emotions* (pp. 91–115). New York: The Guilford Press.

Crane, T. (1992). 'The Nonconceptual Content of Experience'. In T. Crane (ed.), *The Contents of Experience: Essays on Perception*. Cambridge: Cambridge University Press.

——(1998). 'Intentionality as the Mark of the Mental'. In A. O'Hear (ed.), *Contemporary Issues in the Philosophy of Mind* (pp. 229–51). Cambridge: Cambridge University Press.

——(2001). *Elements of Mind: An Introduction to the Philosophy of Mind*. New York: Oxford University Press.

——(2007). 'Intentionalism'. In A. Beckermann and B. McLaughlin (eds.), *The Oxford Handbook to the Philosophy of Mind* (pp. 474–93). New York: Oxford University Press.

Dainton, B. (2000). *Stream of Consciousness: Unity and Continuity in Conscious Experience*. New York: Routledge.

Damasio, A. (2000). *The Feeling of What Happens: Body and Emotion in the Making of Consciousness*. New York: Harcourt Brace.

Damasio, A. R., Grabowski, T. J., Bechara, A., Damasio, H., Ponto, L. L., Parvizi, J., and Hichwaet, R. D. (2000). 'Subcortical and Cortical Brain Activity during the Feeling of Self-Generated Emotions'. *Nature Neuroscience* 3.10, 1049–56.

Dancy, J. (1993). *Moral Reasons*. Cambridge, MA: Blackwell.

——(2004). *Ethics Without Principles*. New York: Oxford University Press.

Danielsson, S. and Olson, J. (2007). 'Brentano and the Buck-Passers'. *Mind* 106, 511–22.

D'Arms, J. (2005). 'Two Arguments for Sentimentalism'. *Philosophical Issues* 15, 1–21.

D'Arms, J. and Jacobson, D. (2000). 'The Moralistic Fallacy: On the "Appropriateness" of Emotions'. *Philosophy and Phenomenological Research* 61.1, 65–90.

——(2010). 'Demystifying Sensibilities: Sentimental Value and the Instability of Affect'. In P. Goldie (ed.), *The Oxford Handbook of Philosophy of Emotion* (pp. 585–613). New York: Oxford University Press.

Darwin, C. (1872/1998). *The Expression of the Emotions in Man and Animals* (P. Ekman, ed.). New York: Oxford University Press.

Deigh, J. (1994). 'Cognitivism in the Theory of Emotions'. *Ethics* 104, 824–54.

Deonna, J. (2006). 'Emotion, Perception, and Perspective'. *Dialectica* 60.1, 29–46.

Deonna, J. and Scherer, K. (2010). 'The Case of the Disappearing Intentional Object: Constraints on a Definition of Emotion'. *Emotion Review* 2.1, 44–52.

Deonna, J. and Teroni, F. (2009). 'Taking Affective Explanations to Heart'. *Social Science Information* 48.3, 359–77.

——(2012). 'From Justified Emotions to Justified Evaluative Judgments'. *Dialogue*.

Deonna, J., Rodogno, R., and Teroni, F. (2011). *In Defense of Shame: The Faces of an Emotion*. New York: Oxford University Press.

Descartes, R. (1649/1989). *The Passions of the Soul* (transl. by S. H. Voss). Indianapolis: Hackett.

De Sousa, R. (1987). *The Rationality of Emotion*. Cambridge, MA: MIT Press.

Dewey, J. (1895). 'The Theory of Emotion. (2) The Significance of Emotions'. *Psychological Review* 2, 13–32.

Dixon, T. (2003). *From Passions to Emotions: The Creation of a Secular Psychological Category*. Cambridge: Cambridge University Press.

Dokic, J. and Lemaire, S. (2012). 'Are Emotions Perceptions of Value?' *Dialogue*.

Döring, S. (2007). 'Affective Perception and Rational Motivation'. *Dialectica* 61.3, 363–94.

——(2009). 'The Logic of Emotional Experience: Non-Inferentiality and the Problem of Conflict Without Contradiction'. *Emotion Review* 1, 240–47.

——(in press). 'From Buck-Passing to No Priority: Towards a Sentimentalist Account of Value'. In S. Roeser and C. Todd (eds.), *Emotions and Values*. Oxford: Oxford University Press.

Doris, J. (2002). *Lack of Character: Personality and Moral Behavior*. Cambridge: Cambridge University Press.

Dretske, F. (1981). *Knowledge and the Flow of Information*. Cambridge, MA: MIT Press.

——(2006). 'Perception Without Awareness'. In T. Szabo Gendler and J. Hawthorne (eds.), *Perceptual Awareness* (pp. 147–80). Oxford: Oxford University Press.

Ekman, P. (1972). *Emotions in the Human Face*. New York: Pergamon Press.

——(1997). 'Basic Emotions'. In T. Dalgleish and T. Power (eds.), *The Handbook of Cognition and Emotion* (pp. 45–60). New York: John Wiley and Sons.

——(2003). *Emotions Revealed: Recognizing Faces and Feelings to Improve Communication and Emotional Life*. New York: Times Books.

Elgin, C. (1996). *Considered Judgment*. Princeton, NJ: Princeton University Press.

——(2008). 'Emotion and Understanding'. In G. Brun, U. Doğuoğlu, and D. Kuenzle (eds.), *Epistemology and Emotions* (pp. 33–49). Aldershot: Ashgate.

Ellsworth, P. C. (1994). 'William James and Emotion: A Century of Fame Worth a Century of Misunderstanding?'. *Psychological Review* 101.2, 222–29.

Ellsworth, P. C. and Scherer, K. (2003). 'Appraisal Processes in Emotion'. In R. J. Davidson, H. Goldsmith, and K. R. Scherer (eds.), *Handbook of Affective Sciences* (pp. 572–95). New York: Oxford University Press.

Elster, J. (1999). *Alchemies of the Mind: Rationality and the Emotions*. New York: Cambridge University Press.

Ewing, A. C. (1947). *The Definition of Good*. London: Hyperion Press.

——(1959). *Second Thoughts in Moral Philosophy*. London: Routledge.

Faucher, L. and Tappolet, C. (2002). 'Fear and the Focus of Attention'. *Consciousness and Emotion* 3.2, 105–44.

——(eds.) (2006). *The Modularity of Emotions. Canadian Journal of Philosophy*, supp. Vol. 32.

Feldman Barrett, L., Niedenthal, P. and Winkielman, P. (eds.) (2005). *Emotions and Consciousness*. New York: The Guilford Press.

Fodor, J. (1983). *The Modularity of Mind*. Cambridge, MA: MIT Press.

Frank, R. (1988). *Passions Within Reason: The Strategic Role of Emotions*. New York: Norton.

Frijda, N. (1986). *The Emotions*. Cambridge: Cambridge University Press.

——(2007). *The Laws of Emotion*. Mahwah, NJ: Lawrence Erlbaum.

Gibbard, A. (1990). *Wise Choices, Apt Feelings: A Theory of Normative Judgment*. Cambridge, MA: Harvard University Press.

Goldie, P. (2000). *The Emotions: A Philosophical Exploration*. Oxford: Oxford University Press.

——(2004a). *On Personality*. New York: Routledge.

——(2004b). 'Emotion, Feeling and Knowledge of the World'. In R. Solomon (ed.), *Thinking about Feeling* (pp. 91–106). New York: Oxford University Press.

——(2007). 'Seeing What is the Kind Thing to Do: Perception and Emotion in Morality'. *Dialectica* 61.3, 347–61.

——(2008). 'Misleading Emotions'. In G. Brun, U. Doğuoğlu, and D. Kuenzle (eds.), *Epistemology and the Emotions* (pp. 149–65). Aldershot: Ashgate.

——(2009). 'Getting Feelings into Emotional Experience in the Right Way'. *Emotion Review* 1.3, 232–39.

Goldman, A. H. (1976). 'Appearing as Irreducible in Perception'. *Philosophy and Phenomenological Research* 37.2, 147–64.

Goldstein, I. (2003). 'Are Emotions Feelings? A Further Look at Hedonic Theories of Emotions'. *Consciousness and Emotion* 3, 21–33.

Gordon, R. (1987). *The Structure of Emotions: Investigations in Cognitive Philosophy*. Cambridge: Cambridge University Press.

Graver, F. (2007). *Stoicism and Emotion*. Chicago: University of Chicago Press.

Green, O. H. (1992). *The Emotions: A Philosophical Theory*. Dordrecht: Kluwer.

Greenspan, P. S. (1988). *Emotions and Reasons*. New York: Routledge.

Griffiths, P. E. (1997). *What Emotions Really Are: The Problem of Psychological Categories*. Chicago: University of Chicago Press.

Gross, J. J. (ed.) (2007). *Handbook of Emotion Regulation*. New York: The Guilford Press.

Haidt, J. (2003). 'The Moral Emotions'. In R. J. Davidson, K. R. Scherer, and H. H. Goldsmith (eds.), *Handbook of Affective Sciences* (pp. 852–70). New York: Oxford University Press.

Harman, G. (1990). 'The Intrinsic Quality of Experience'. In J. E. Tomberlin (ed.), *Philosophical Perspectives 4: Action Theory and the Philosophy of Mind* (pp. 31–52). Atascadero, CA: Ridgeview.

——(1999). 'Moral Philosophy Meets Social Psychology: Virtue Ethics and the Fundamental Attribution Error'. *Proceedings of the Aristotelian Society* 99, 315–31.

Hatzimoysis, A. (2007). 'The Case Against Unconscious Emotions'. *Analysis* 67.4, 292–99.

Helm, B. (2001). *Emotional Reason: Deliberation, Motivation, and the Nature of Value*. Cambridge: Cambridge University Press.

——(2010). *Love, Friendship, and the Self: Intimacy, Identification, and the Social Nature of Persons*. New York: Oxford University Press.

Hobbes, T. (1668/1994). *Leviathan* (E. Curley ed.). Indianapolis: Hackett.

Hudson, S. (1980). 'Character Traits and Desires'. *Ethics* 90.4, 539–49.

Humberstone, L. (1992). 'Direction of Fit'. *Mind* 101.401, 59–83.

Hume, D. (1975). *Enquiries Concerning Human Understanding and Concerning the Principles of Morals* (L. A. Selby-Bigge ed.). Oxford: Oxford University Press.

Jackson, F. (1998). *From Metaphysics to Ethics: A Defence of Conceptual Analysis*. Oxford: Oxford University Press.

Jäger, C. and Bartsch, A. (2006). 'Meta-Emotions'. *Grazer Philosophische Studien* 73, 179–204.

James, W. (1884). 'What is an Emotion?'. *Mind* 9, 188–205.

——(1890/1950). *The Principles of Psychology*. New York: Dover.

Johnston, M. (2001). 'The Authority of Affect'. *Philosophy and Phenomenological Research* 53, 181–214.

Jones, K. (2003). 'Emotion, Weakness of Will, and the Normative Conception of Agency'. In A. Hatzimoysis (ed.), *The Philosophy of Emotions* (pp. 181–99). Cambridge: Cambridge University Press.

——(2006). 'Metaethics and Emotions Research: A Response to Prinz'. *Philosophical Explorations* 9.1, 45–53

Kenny, A. (1963). *Action, Emotion and Will*. London: Routledge and Kegan Paul.

Kriegel, U. (2012). 'Towards a New Feeling Theory of Emotion'. *European Journal of Philosophy*.

Lacewing, M. (2007). 'Do Unconscious Emotions Involve Unconscious Feelings?'. *Philosophical Psychology* 20.1, 81–104.

Lambie, J. A. and Marcel, A. J. (2002). 'Consciousness and the Variety of Emotion Experience: A Theoretical Framework'. *Psychological Review* 109.2, 219–59.

Lance, M. and Tanesini, A. (2004). 'Emotion and Rationality'. In M. Ezcurdia, R. Stainton, and C. Viger (eds.), *New Essays in the Philosophy of Mind and Language* (pp. 275–95). *Canadian Journal of Philosophy* suppl. Vol. 30.

Lange, C. G. (1922). *The Emotions* (transl. by I.A. Haupt). Baltimore, MD: Williams and Wilkins.

Lazarus, R. S. (1991). *Emotion and Adaptation*. New York: Oxford University Press.

LeDoux, J. (1996). *The Emotional Brain: The Mysterious Underpinnings of Emotional Life*. New York: Simon and Schuster.

Leighton, S. R. (1984). 'Feeling and Emotion'. *Review of Metaphysics* 38, 303–20.

Lewis, D. (1989). 'Dispositional Theories of Values'. *Proceedings of the Aristotelian Society* Supp. Vol. 63, 113–37.

Louise, J. (2009). 'Correct Responses and the Priority of the Normative'. *Ethical Theory and Moral Practice* 12.4, 345–64.

Lyons, W. (1980). *Emotion*. Cambridge: Cambridge University Press.

Maiese, M. (2011). *Embodiment, Emotion, and Cognition*. New York: Palgrave Macmillan.

Mandler, G. (1975). *Mind and Emotion*. New York: Wiley.

Marks, J. (1982). 'A Theory of Emotion'. *Philosophical Studies* 42, 227–42.

McDowell, J. (1979). 'Virtue and Reason'. *The Monist* 62, 331–50.

——(1985). 'Values and Secondary Qualities'. In T. Honderich (ed.), *Morality and Objectivity* (pp. 110–29). London: Routledge.

McLean, P. D. (1993). 'Cerebral Evolution of Emotion'. In M. Lewis and J. M. Haviland (eds.), *Handbook of Emotions* (pp. 67–83). New York: The Guilford Press.

Millikan, R. G. (1987). *Language, Thought, and Other Biological Categories: New Foundations for Realism*. Cambridge, MA: MIT Press.

Montague, M. (2007). 'Against Propositionalism'. *Nous* 41:3, 503–18.

Moore, G. E. (1903). *Principia Ethica*. Cambridge: Cambridge University Press.

Morton, A. (1980). *Frames of Mind: Constraints on the Common-sense Conception of the Mental*. Oxford: Oxford University Press.

Mulligan, K. (1998). 'From Appropriate Emotions to Values'. *The Monist* 81.1, 161–88.

——(2007). 'Intentionality, Knowledge and Formal Objects'. *Disputatio* 2.23, 205–28.

——(2010). 'Emotions and Values'. In P. Goldie (ed.), *The Oxford Handbook of Philosophy of Emotion* (pp. 475–500). New York: Oxford University Press.

Nagel, T. (1970). *The Possibility of Altruism*. Oxford: Oxford Unversity Press.

Neu, J. (2000). *A Tear is an Intellectual Thing: The Meanings of Emotion*. New York: Oxford University Press.

Nichols, S. (2004). *Sentimental Rules: On the Natural Foundations of Moral Judgment*. New York: Oxford University Press.

Nisbett, R. E. and Ross, L. (1980). *Human Inference: Strategies and Shortcoming of Social Judgment*. Englewood Cliffs, NJ: Prentice-Hall.

Nussbaum, M. C. (1994). *The Therapy of Desire: Theory and Practice in Hellenistic Ethics*. Princeton, NJ: Princeton University Press.

——(2003). *Upheavals of Thought: The Intelligence of Emotions*. Cambridge: Cambridge University Press.

——(2004). 'Emotions as Judgments of Value and Importance'. In R. C. Solomon (ed.), *Thinking About Feeling: Contemporary Philosophers on Emotions* (pp. 183–99). New York: Oxford University Press.

Oddie, G. (2005). *Value, Reality and Desire*. New York: Oxford University Press.

Panksepp, J. (2000). 'Emotion as a Natural Kind Within the Brain'. In M. Lewis and J. M. Haviland-Jones (eds.), *Handbook of Emotions* (pp. 137–50). New York: The Guilford Press.

Parfit, D. (2006). *Climbing the Mountain*. Unpublished manuscript.

Peacocke, C. (1996). 'Précis of *A Study of Concepts*'. *Philosophy and Phenomenological Research* 56.2, 407–11.

——(2004). *The Realm of Reason*. New York: Oxford University Press.

Pitcher, G. (1971). *A Theory of Perception*. Princeton, NJ: Princeton University Press.

Platts, M. (1991). *Moral Realities: An Essay in Philosophical Psychology*. London: Routledge.

Plutchik, R. (1980). *Emotion: A Psychoevolutionary Synthesis*. New York: Harper and Row.

——(2001). 'The Nature of Emotions'. *American Scientist* 89, 344–50.

Pollock, J. (1974). *Knowledge and Justification*. Princeton, NJ: Princeton University Press.

Pollock, J. and Cruz, J. (1999). *Contemporary Theories of Knowledge*. Lanham, MD: Rowman and Littlefield.

Prinz, J. (2004). *Gut Reactions: A Perceptual Theory of Emotions*. New York: Oxford University Press.

——(2005). 'Emotions, Embodiment, and Awareness'. In L. Feldman Barrett, P. Niedenthal and P. Winkielman (eds.), *Emotions and Consciousness* (pp. 363–383). New York: The Guilford Press.

——(2006). 'The Emotional Basis of Moral Judgments'. *Philosophical Explorations* 9.1, 29–43.

——(2007). *The Emotional Construction of Morals*. New York: Oxford University Press.

——(2010). 'For Valence'. *Emotion Review* 2.1, 5–13.

Pritchard, D. (2005). *Epistemic Luck*. Oxford: Oxford University Press.

Pugmire, D. (1998). *Rediscovering Emotions*. Edinburgh: Edinburgh University Press.

——(2006). 'Emotion and Emotion Science'. *European Journal of Analytic Philosophy* 2.1, 7–27.

Rabinowicz, W. and Rønnow-Rasmussen, T. (2004). 'The Strike of the Demon: On Fitting Pro-attitudes and Value'. *Ethics* 114, 391–423.

Ratcliffe, M. (2005). 'Willam James on Emotion and Intentionality'. *International Journal of Philosophical Studies* 13.2, 179–202.

——(2008). *Feelings of Being: Phenomenology, Psychiatry and the Sense of Reality*. Oxford: Oxford University Press.

Rawls, J. (1971). *A Theory of Justice*. Cambridge, MA: Harvard University Press.

Récanati, F. (2007). *Perspectival Thought: A Plea for (Moderate) Relativism*. New York: Oxford University Press.

Reisenzein, R. (2009). 'Emotions as Metarepresentational States of Mind: Naturalizing the Belief-Desire Theory of Emotion'. *Cognitive Systems Research* 10, 6–20.

Reisner, A. (2009). 'Abandoning the Buck Passing Analysis of Final Value'. *Ethical Theory and Moral Practice* 12.4, 379–95.

Roberts, R. (2003). *Emotions: An Essay in Aid of Moral Psychology*. Cambridge: Cambridge University Press.

Roberts, R. C. and Wood, W. J. (2007). *Intellectual Virtues: An Essay in Regulative Epistemology*. Oxford: Oxford University Press.

Robinson, J. (2005). *Deeper than Reason: Emotion and its Role in Literature, Music, and Art*. New York: Oxford University Press.

Roeser, S. (2011). *Moral Emotions and Intuitions*. New York: Palgrave Macmillan.

Ruse, M. and Wilson, O. (1986). 'Moral Philosophy as Applied Science'. *Philosophy* 61.236, 173–92.

Russell, J. (2003). 'Core Affect and the Construction of Emotions'. *Psychological Review* 110, 145–72.

Salmela, M. (2006). 'True Emotions'. *Philosophical Quarterly* 56.224, 382–405.

——(2011). 'Can Emotions be Modelled on Perception?' *Dialectica* 65.1, 1–29.

Sartre, J.-P. (1948). *Esquisse d'une théorie des émotions*. Paris: Hermann.

Scanlon, T. M. (1998). *What We Owe to Each Other*. Cambridge, MA: Harvard University Press.

Schachter, S. and Singer, J. (1962). 'Cognitive, Social, and Physiological Determinants of Emotional States'. *Psychological Review* 69, 379–99.

Scherer, K. R. (2001). 'Appraisal Considered as a Process of Multilevel Sequential Checking'. In K. Scherer, A. Schorr, and T. Johnson (eds.), *Appraisal Processes in Emotion Theory, Methods, Research* (pp. 92–120). Oxford: Oxford University Press.

——(2009). 'The Dynamic Architecture of Emotion: Evidence for the Component Model Process'. *Cognition and Emotion* 23.7, 1307–51.

Scherer, K. R. and Ellgring, H. (2007). 'Multimodal Expression of Emotion: Affect Programs or Componential Appraisal Patterns?'. *Emotion* 7.1, 158–71.

Schroeder, M. (2007). *Slaves of the Passions*. New York: Oxford University Press.

Schroeder, T. (2004). *Three Faces of Desire*. New York: Oxford University Press.

——(2006). 'An Unexpected Pleasure'. In L. Faucher and C. Tappolet (eds.), *Canadian Journal of Philosophy*, supp. Vol. 32, *The Modularity of Emotions* (pp. 255–72).

——(2009). 'Desire'. *Stanford Encyclopedia of Philosophy (Winter 2009 Edition)*, E. N. Zalta (ed.), http://plato.stanford.edu/archives/win2009/entries/desire/ (accessed October 20, 2011).

Schueler, G. F. (1995). *Desire: Its Role in Practical Reason and the Explanation of Action*. Cambridge, MA: MIT Press.

——(2003). *Reasons and Purposes: Human Rationality and the Teleological Explanation of Action*. New York: Oxford University Press.

Searle, J. (1983). *Intentionality: An Essay in the Philosophy of Mind*. New York: Cambridge University Press.

Siegel, S. (2006). 'Which Properties are Represented in Perception?'. In T. Gendler Szabo and J. Hawthorne (eds.), *Perceptual Experience* (pp. 481–503). Oxford: Oxford University Press.

Slaby, I. (2008). 'Affective Intentionality and the Feeling Body'. *Phenomenology and the Cognitive Sciences* 7.4, 429–44.

Smith, A. (1790/1976). *The Theory of Moral Sentiments* (D. D. Raphael and A. L. Macfie eds.). Oxford: Clarendon Press.

Smith, M. (1989). 'Dispositional Theories of Values'. *Proceedings of the Aristotelian Society* Supp. Vol. 63, 89–111.

——(1994). *The Moral Problem*. Oxford: Blackwell.

Soldati, G. (2008). 'Transparenz der Gefühle'. In B. Merker (ed.), *Emotionen Interdisziplinär* (pp. 257–80). Paderborn: Mentis.

Solomon, R. (1973). 'Emotion and Choice'. *The Review of Metaphysics* 27.1, 20–41.

——(1993). *The Passions: Emotions and the Meaning of Life*. Indianapolis: Hackett.

——(2001). 'Back to Basics: On the Very Idea of "Basic Emotions"'. In R. Solomon, *Not Passion's Slave* (pp. 115–42). New York: Oxford University Press.

——(2002). 'Thoughts and Feelings: What is a "Cognitive" Theory of the Emotions and Does it Neglect Affectivity?'. In A. Hatzimoysis (ed.), *The Philosophy of Emotions* (pp. 1–18). Cambridge: Cambridge University Press.

——(2003). 'Against Valence ("Positive" and "Negative" Emotions)'. In R. Solomon, *Not Passion's Slave* (pp. 162–77). New York: Oxford University Press.

Sorabji, R. (2003). *Emotion and Peace of Mind: From Stoic Agitation to Christian Temptation*. New York: Oxford University Press.

Stocker, M. (1983). 'Psychic Feelings: Their Importance and Irreducibility'. *Australasian Journal of Philosophy* 61, 5–26.

Strandberg, C. (2008). 'Particularism and Supervenience'. In R. Shafer-Landau (ed.), *Oxford Studies in Metaethics Vol. 3* (pp. 129–58). New York: Oxford University Press.

Strawson, G. (2010). *Mental Reality*, second edition. Cambridge, MA: MIT Press.

Stroud, S. and Tappolet, C. (eds.) (2003). *Weakness of Will and Practical Irrationality*. New York: Oxford University Press.

Tappolet, C. (2000). *Emotions et valeurs*. Paris: Presses Universitaires de France.

——(2003). 'Emotions and the Intelligibility of Akratic Action'. In S. Stroud and C. Tappolet (eds.), *Weakness of Will and Practical Irrationality* (pp. 97–121). New York: Oxford University Press.

——(2011). 'Values and Emotions: Neo-sentimentalism's Prospects'. In C. Bagnoli (ed.), *Morality and the Emotions* (pp. 117–134). New York: Oxford University Press.

Tenenbaum, S. (2007). *Appearances of the Good: An Essay on the Nature of Practical Reason*. Cambridge: Cambridge University Press.

Teroni, F. (2007). 'Emotions and Formal Objects'. *Dialectica* 61.3, 395–415.

Tracy, J. L., Robins, R. W., and Tangney, J. P. (2007) (eds.). *The Self-conscious Emotions: Theory and Research*. New York: The Guilford Press.

Tye, M. (2008). 'The Experience of Emotion: An Intentionalist Theory'. *Revue Internationale de Philosophie* 243, 25–50.

Wall, D. (2009). 'Are There Passive Desires?'. *Dialectica* 63.2, 133–55.

Wallace, R. J. (2010). 'Reasons, Values and Agent-Relativity'. *Dialectica* 64.4, 503–28.

Walton, K. L. (1990). *Mimesis as Make-Believe: On the Foundation of the Representational Arts*. Cambridge, MA: Harvard University Press.

Wedgwood, R. (2001). 'Sensing Values?'. *Philosophy and Phenomenological Research* 63.1, 215–223.

Whiting, D. (2011). 'The Feeling Theory of Emotions and Object-Directed Emotions'. *European Journal of Philosophy* 19.2, 281–303.

——(2012). 'Are Emotions Perceptual Experiences of Value?' *Ratio*.

Williams, B. (1973). *Problems of the Self*. New York: Cambridge University Press.

Wiggins, D. (1975–76). 'Deliberation and Practical Reason'. *Proceedings of the Aristotelian Society* 76, 43–49.

——(1987). 'A Sensible Subjectivism?'. In *Needs, Values, Truth: Essays in the Philosophy of Value*. Oxford: Blackwell.

Wollheim, R. (1999). *On the Emotions*. New Haven, CT: Yale University Press.

Zagzebski, L. (2003). 'Emotion and Moral Judgment'. *Philosophy and Phenomenological Research* 66.1, 104–24.

# Index